DON'T STOP BELIEVING

DON'T
STOP
BELIEVING
A Life I Lived Inside

LOLA MAY GROVES

Copyright © 2015 by Lola May Groves.

Library of Congress Control Number: 2015919578
ISBN: Hardcover   978-1-5144-2926-6
             Softcover   978-1-5144-2925-9
             eBook   978-1-5144-2924-2

All rights reserved. No part of this book may be reproduced or transmitted in any form or by any means, electronic or mechanical, including photocopying, recording, or by any information storage and retrieval system, without permission in writing from the copyright owner.

Any people depicted in stock imagery provided by Thinkstock are models, and such images are being used for illustrative purposes only.
Certain stock imagery © Thinkstock.

Print information available on the last page.

Rev. date: 11/24/2015

To order additional copies of this book, contact:
Xlibris
1-888-795-4274
www.Xlibris.com
Orders@Xlibris.com

726798

This book is dedicated to all the girls who think their lives are so bad that it isn't worth living. Just remember that you can make changes to improve your life. Only you can do it. Don't blame others for your bad luck; just make some changes and see your life improve so you can live a happy life.

Contents

Chapter 1 1
Chapter 2 4
Chapter 3 10
Chapter 4 14
Chapter 5 16
Chapter 6 18
Chapter 7 21
Chapter 8 28
Chapter 9 32
Chapter 10 38
Chapter 11 42
Chapter 12 45
Chapter 13 52
Chapter 14 55
Chapter 15 61
Chapter 16 65
Chapter 17 68
Chapter 18 70
Chapter 19 71
Chapter 20 74
Chapter 21 76
Chapter 22 78
Chapter 23 81

INTRODUCTION

Katie Macollin grew up a sad little girl and very unloved. A devoted boyfriend kept Katie on board and may have prevented her from committing suicide. Many teens have committed suicide because their lives were so unbearable.

Katie kept wondering if her life would change for the better. She decided to make the changes happen by pushing forward with her career. After a while, Katie realized that her parents do love her. She learned she had more friends than she thought she had.

Believing that her boyfriend would come home from college to marry Katie, she kept her spirits up and believed they would have a future together.

Chapter 1

I am Katie Macollin. I am eighteen years old and about to graduate from high school and pursue a career as a medical assistant. I have always admired people working in the medical field and thought I could help my community by working at a clinic. If I went to Des Moines Community College, I could live at home so it wouldn't cost as much as living in a dorm on campus. I have a week of final exams to finish my training then do my clinicals, or on-the-job training. I would have to do some inquiring at the college to see what is available for financing my education.

The Macollin family owns a horse farm about five miles outside of Des Moines, Iowa. My dad, Bob, trains and boards horses for a living. The farm belonged to my grandfather Macollin until he decided to move to the city. My mom, Cindy, works at the First National Bank in Des Moines, where she has been a teller for a number of years and has been recently promoted to vice president. She was very excited about her promotion. Greg, my oldest brother, has been married to his high school sweetheart, April, for about one year. They live on a neighboring farm, where they raise dairy cows. The farm is owned by April's parents, and April's dad is teaching Greg the ropes so one day he can take over the farm. April is an only child, so they want Greg and April to inherit the property. I have another older brother, Dan, who still lives at home. He is engaged to his girlfriend, Lori. The wedding is a couple of years down the road. Lori and Dan are both in college and want to finish before taking on wedded bliss. Dan is studying to be a teacher, and Lori is studying to be a social worker.

I'm not very close to my parents, and they haven't shown much affection to me in a very long time. I can't understand what I had done to cause my parents to practically disown their only daughter. Maybe they just wanted boys. Since I had been about ten years old, I helped around the house, cleaning, laundering, and eventually learning to cook. I have felt more like a maid than a daughter, while my mother worked outside of the home and went to meetings and club activities. I felt like I was living the whole Cinderella story. No matter what I did, it wasn't good enough to win their love and affection. It's a good thing I don't have any younger siblings or I would have had to babysit also. I have been looking forward to getting out of the house where I have felt like an outsider for a long time. Maybe I was adopted, although no one had told me any different.

I sat, thinking back to my lonely grade school and high school days, and wondered if there is a better life for me somewhere down the road. After careful thought, I put a smile on my face and thought, *I am an adult now, and I can change the direction of my life, and that's what I am going to do. I have to make the change in my life, no one else can do it. I will have a talk with the guidance counselor after school and see what she has to offer.*

As I headed to the counselor's office, I was full of hope for my future. I would talk to Mrs. Arnoldson about going to the community college to become a medical assistant. Hopefully, I could arrange for some financial assistance.

I knocked on Mrs. Arnoldson's door, and she looked up with a big smile on her face. "Come in, Katie, what can I do for you today? You are about to graduate, and I haven't talked with you about what you want to do after graduation. I was thinking about looking you up to see if I can help you make a decision about your future."

I told Mrs. Arnoldson that I was thinking of becoming a medical assistant and working at one of the clinics in the Des Moines area. "I think being a medical assistant will be very fulfilling, and I can go to the community college instead of a major college. I don't have funding to go to a major college."

"I think it is wonderful that you want to go to the community college to get a degree. I will help you all I can with getting your paperwork done and setting up a financial aid. I will call over there right now and get the ball rolling. How about that?" Mrs. Arnoldson was a nice lady and always wanted to help students out. Mrs. Arnoldson picked up the phone and made her call as I sat nervously, hoping everything would work out.

When Mrs. Arnoldson hung up the phone, she looked up at me with a smile on her face. "I have good news for you. You can go over tomorrow to talk with an adviser that will tell you your options and help you sign up for classes." She handed me some brochures to read about the medical assistant program. I couldn't wait to read them and go over to the school the next day to sign up.

When I got home, I started supper for my family and read the brochures. I was so excited, glancing at the classes I would have to take. *These classes sound like a lot of fun. If only I could start tomorrow. This has to happen for me. I will make this happen for me.*

I thought my life was definitely taking a turn for the better. Actually, I felt pretty lucky right then. I had a boyfriend, Mark Johnson, who loves me and had always been there for me since we were very young. I also had Mark's sister, Amy, and his parents. It seemed they were always there when I needed them and always looked out for my well-being. I didn't know where my life would be now if I didn't have them to keep encouraging me. I finally realized what it was like to have devoted friends to rely on. I thanked God every day that he sent the Johnson family to look out for me.

Chapter 2

Finally, I completed my high school courses, and it was graduation night. I went over to Amy's to get ready to go to the school. It was a warm evening, so I wore shorts and a tank top because with the robe over our clothes, it would be quite warm. I took pants and a dressy shirt with me for after graduation. The graduation party started at ten, so we would change for that. The party would go all night.

Amy's parents dropped us off at the door of the high school at six thirty. They would find a parking spot and then make their way to the gymnasium for the graduation ceremony. We were excited to be graduating. Little did we realize there was a big whole world out there to face. We should have been scared, but we were too excited tonight to even think about what lay ahead of us. We were ready to face the world; we were graduating!

I knew Mark was coming home for the ceremony. He had called to ask what time the ceremony would start. I told him if he was too busy with his schoolwork, I would understand. Mark was attending Iowa State University, majoring in law. He was working very hard because he wanted to graduate early. Mark was anxious to practice law. He told me he was coming because this night was very special for me, and he wanted to share in my joy. He also wanted to be there for Amy as they were very close. It would be wonderful to see him again. We could spend most of the weekend together. We treasured what little time we had on the rare weekends Mark came home.

At seven o'clock, we marched into the auditorium. There were a lot of people here. I would never find any of my family, if they did come. Mom and Dad didn't tell me if they were coming or not. I didn't really expect them to, but it would be nice if they could share in my accomplishment. I knew Mark and his parents would be here because Amy was graduating too. I fidgeted and turned to see if I could see Mark in the audience. I couldn't wait for the ceremony to be over so we could be together.

"Where is he?" I asked Amy, who was sitting beside me. "I hope he was able to make it. Maybe he decided he needed to stay at college after all. Maybe he got stuck in traffic, which is always busy in the evening with so many people coming home from work."

Amy was looking around too. "If he said he would be here, he'll be here. He is a man of his word, Katie. He would not let you down on such a special day. Look, I see Mom, Dad, and Phil, straight back and about ten rows up. I don't see Mark with them though, but don't worry, he will be here.

"I know, I'm just excited to see him," I expressed as the ceremony started.

The ceremony was wonderful. The speakers were very enlightening and spoke of our future after high school. After all the speakers were finished speaking, we filed up to go across the stage to receive our diplomas. I felt so proud that this day had finally come.

At last, the ceremony was over, and we had our diplomas. When everyone was back to their seat, we stood up and threw our hats in the air and screamed at the top of our lungs. The principal, superintendent, and the other speakers started down the aisle, and we followed. We lined up along the wall of the corridor to await our families.

I waited anxiously to see if Mark had made it home from college. At last, Joy, Paul, Phil, and Mark found us. They all hugged and congratulated us on graduating.

As Mark and I hugged, I whispered to him, "I didn't see you sitting with your parents and was so afraid that you hadn't made it home. I am so glad you did!"

"Well, traffic was a nightmare, and I dropped my buddy, Steve, off at his parents' house before coming to the school. Since we were both coming home, we figured we would drive together instead of taking two cars. I thought I had it all planned out time-wise, but I ran a little short on time, but I got here right as the ceremony started."

To my surprise, my parents soon joined us. I could hardly believe it. I wanted them here, but I didn't want to be disappointed if they hadn't come. Greg, April, Dan, and his girlfriend, Lori, were also with them. Could the night get any better? They had all come to see me graduate.

After several hugs and kisses, Joy announced that they had reservations at Willow Creek Inn for a late dinner and celebration. Everyone was invited, but only Mom and Dad from my side said they were coming. Mark asked if I wanted to ride with him. Of course I said yes. As always, we were very happy to see each other, and we joined hands and headed for his car. We all left for the restaurant, which took us a while with the traffic so heavy. I didn't mind though; I was able to be with my sweetheart. We talked and laughed all the way to the restaurant.

Mark seemed really happy; he kept smiling at me. I asked, "What are you smiling at?"

"I'm just glad to see you. You look a lot smarter and more grown up all of a sudden. Somehow, graduating makes a person into an adult," he told me, still smiling.

We ordered our drinks and dinner. After the waitress left, Mark's parents handed me an envelope. I thought it was just a graduation card, but when I opened it, $100 fell onto the table, and I gasped. "Oh my gosh, this is too much. Thank you very much!" I was ecstatic!

I hugged them and was almost in tears. Mark's parents were always very good to me, and I loved them almost more than my own parents.

Then my dad pulled an envelope from his pocket and handed it to me. He smiled at me as I opened it. "Congratulations, sweetie. I hope you can use some extra cash for college." Inside was $200. I was so amazed I was speechless. I managed to thank and hug them too. I couldn't hold the tears back. I just couldn't believe this night could be so great.

Amy was also given her graduation cards with money in them. Paul and Joy gave Amy $200, and my parents gave her $100 even though she was having a graduation party in two weeks. My parents hadn't even asked if I wanted a party. What a surprise there.

Mark was still smiling from ear to ear and couldn't sit still. I knew something was up, and I kept looking at him in wonder. At last, he got up from his chair and knelt on one knee and took my hands in his. "Katie, I have a gift for you too." He was pulling a jewelry box out of his pocket. Looking lovingly into my eyes, he said, "I was wondering if you would do me the honor of being my wife. I love you and want us to spend the rest of our lives together."

"Oh yes, I will marry you, Mark," I cried out to him. "I love you too." There was a whole lot of hugging and kissing going on then. I knew we had talked about getting married someday, but I didn't expect it yet with Mark still in college. I was so surprised I couldn't stop smiling.

Paul ordered a bottle of champagne to celebrate our wonderful evening. When the champagne arrived, the waiter poured the adults each a glass and left. Phil poured; Amy and I just got a sip as we were underage. It probably wouldn't be good to go to our all-night graduation party with booze on our breath. Our parents thought that under the circumstances, one sip would be acceptable.

I felt very delighted that Mark promised to love me forever and would wait for me if I would wait for him. That was way into the future, as Mark had about two years of college left. We wanted each other, and we could make it work. I wasn't used to having good things happen to me, but maybe things were changing for the better.

My mom hugged me and said, "Congratulations." My dad stepped in front of me and hugged me and said, "I am very proud of you for graduating from high school, and congratulations on your engagement. I know you and Mark will be very happy together. I am so proud of you!"

I couldn't believe my ears. My parents didn't get sentimental and loving. Would wonders never cease?

When we were done eating, Amy and I decided we should probably get over to the school for the overnight graduation party. We were all expected to attend the party. They didn't want us out driving around because in previous years, kids went driving and drinking only to end up in a serious accident. So they decided to make the party mandatory. Since the parties at the school had been started, they hadn't had any accidents on graduation night.

The graduation party was a lot of fun for most of the students. We had records to dance to and lots of food to eat. Several times during the night, they drew names for prizes. Amy won a stereo, and I won a gift certificate of $100 for Walmart.

Amy danced with a lot of boys, but no boys asked me to dance. I was just a wallflower, as usual. Amy, always wanting to make me a part of things, danced a couple of songs with me. Finally, at four o'clock, Amy and I fell asleep on our sleeping bags. We weren't used to staying up all night. I knew I had Saturday to spend with Mark, and I didn't want to spend it sleeping. The time we spent together was too precious.

At eight o'clock, we were awakened by some people bringing in breakfast for us. It was wonderful. Amy and I ate together and then gathered our sleeping bags and clothes to go wait for Mark and Phil by the front door.

Mark and Phil arrived to pick us up right on time. We were all anxious to see one another. We told them about our night as we drove to Amy and Mark's house.

Chapter 3

The day after graduation, I spent the day with Mark, Amy, and Phil. We went for a drive in the country, and then we stopped at a little restaurant for lunch. The four of us played cards when we arrived back at the house. At five o'clock, Mark dropped me off at home to change clothes, as Mark was taking me to the movies that evening.

When I walked into the house, Dad was sitting at the table, going over his books and probably paying bills. He called me over to him. "Hi, Dad, I was really thrilled that you and Mom went to graduation last night. Thank you," I told him.

"It was only right that we go. I know things haven't been the greatest between us. I am sorry for that. I see here that you brought home some brochures for medical assisting. Is this something you plan on pursuing?"

I sat down at the table with my dad and explained. "I thought it would be the cheapest route to go so I could have some college degree. It is cheaper than the university. I need some schooling if I want to get a fairly decent job. Mrs. Arnoldson at the high school helped me with enrollment and financing at the college. I am enrolled to start in late August. If it is okay, I would like to live here while I'm going to school. If not, I will make other arrangements. Just let me know."

Dad went to get a cup of coffee. "Do you want a cup?" he asked. I nodded, and Dad returned to his seat with our coffee. He sat back down and tenderly told me, "It will be fine if you want to stay here, and how expensive are your classes going to be?"

I reluctantly told him what each class would cost. I was afraid he would think they were too expensive, so I never considered going to him for any help because I didn't think I could ask for his help. "I don't know if there will be any extra fees or expenses."

Dad smiled at me and said, "That doesn't sound so bad. I think I can handle it. When do you need the money? You weren't going to ask me to help pay for this, were you? You know you don't have to do everything on your own. We paid for your brothers' college education, why wouldn't we pay for yours?"

Sadly I told Dad, "Over the years, I haven't been top on yours and Mom's list of favorite people. I'm usually ignored, so I didn't think anything had changed. I just figured I would sign up for financial aid so I wouldn't be a burden to you. I will have loans to pay off, but I can do it. I usually don't get help with anything and didn't think college would be any different.

"I have felt like I have been on my own for the last six or so years. Do you even know if I'm home or not? Do you and Mom even care? As long as the cooking, cleaning and laundry gets done, the house is at peace, but if they're not done, I get yelled at. While I'm going to school, I might not have as much time to be your maid. I will do what I can, but my schooling has to come first. My grades suffered in high school because after doing all the work around the house, I didn't have enough time to study and do my assignments. This has to be different. You don't want to pay for classes that I fail in, do you? I want to do well."

I had never told my dad the way I felt before. It felt pretty good to get it off my chest. Maybe I should have done it long ago. Maybe things would have been different. I had tears in my eyes, but I felt like the air had to be cleared between us so we could have some sort of relationship as father and daughter. I think he does love me, but things had gotten so strained between us he didn't know how to fix the problem. I didn't know if there was any fixing, but I felt I had to try. I didn't know what to say until I started talking, and all of a sudden, it came pouring out of my mouth. I didn't know I had such courage.

"I'm very sorry I didn't see this problem before you pointed it out. I guess I was too wrapped up in my horses to pay much attention to my family. I knew you weren't very happy at times, but I didn't take the time to find out why. I'm sorry I didn't make the time to see that you were happy. I'm so sorry you had to go through these years feeling like you weren't loved, because I did and I do love you, Katie. I guess I forgot to show and tell you how much I loved you. I hope it is not too late to make this right. Can I buy you a pony?" Dad looked at me and smiled.

"I think I'm a little too old for a pony, Dad," I said laughingly. "But it is nice to hear you say that you do love me. I felt very alone and unloved growing up, and I didn't think I was wanted, so I just tried to do as I was told and stay out of your way. I figured you and Mom couldn't wait for me to graduate and get out of your hair. It will take some work, but we can work on our relationship, if you have the time. I know you're very busy. I'm sure that hasn't changed, but maybe we can start spending more time together if you want to."

Dad got up from the table and pulled me up to meet him in a hug. He hugged so hard I could hardly breathe. "I would like to spend more time with you, and I will find the time. Maybe we can go horseback riding? Do you remember how to ride? Maybe we can go out to lunch or dinner sometime. Whatever you would like to do, just suggest away and we'll do it. Okay? I bet you could use a car to get to school. How about we go look for a car for you on Monday? It will probably have to be a secondhand car, but if it gets you where you need to go, I think it will be okay. What do you think?"

"I hadn't thought about a car. I have my graduation money to put toward it. It's not much, but it will help. If I get a car, maybe I could get a summer job to pay you back and help with college expenses," I said. "Thanks, Dad, this has meant a lot to me to be able to talk to you today. I have a date with Mark tonight, so I better get ready. I will be home by eleven o'clock."

Dad smiled at me and said, "You know, you have graduated now. I don't think you need to have a curfew. Just be safe tonight and I will be happy."

I hugged Dad again and headed off to my bedroom to get ready for my date.

Chapter 4

Mark picked me up for our date at about six o'clock, and I told him about the conversation I had with my dad. I told him how happy I was that he was going to help me get a car and pay for my college courses. "I want to get a summer job to save some money for gas and insurance for my car. I can do that much," I told Mark, trying to sound like a mature adult now that I had graduated from high school.

Mark took my hands in his and smiled. "It's great that you and your dad talked. It's about time. I hope he doesn't let you down. I'm sorry I can't be here to help you find a car. We should have gone today to look for a car for you, but maybe it is a good thing to do this with your dad. It sounds like the car subject was part of what broke the ice between you and your dad. If he doesn't come through, maybe I can ask my dad to help you. Just keep that in mind. What kind of job are you going to be looking for?"

"I don't know. Maybe I could go to the college and see if they hire help over the summer. I will take whatever I can get. You know what else? I no longer have a curfew. Dad said that I am an adult now and don't need one. What do you think about that?" I said proudly.

"I'm glad that he lifted your curfew, but I don't want to push his buttons and cause him to be upset with you or me. I think it's a good idea to start at the college. I know my college hires quite a few students around the school. It is a big help for students that need some extra money. Maybe you can work a little during school too. I am so proud of you, Katie. You have taken life by storm to make things happen for you, and I guess in a way for me." Mark smiled and hugged me as if he never wanted to let go. Looking me in the eyes, he said, "I hope the next two years go fast so we can start our lives together. I do feel better leaving you now that you and your dad have made peace. I'm very happy for you. I still hate to leave you though. I always feel like I'm leaving a piece of myself behind when I have to leave. It's such an empty feeling. I love you so very much!"

"I love you too. Why don't we take some pictures of each other to look at when we are feeling lonely? I will miss you too, but college is very important. You will have an excellent career when you are done, and that is important for our future. I am very proud of you," I told Mark as he walked me to the door.

When we got to the door, Mark turned me toward him and bent down to kiss me. His kisses were always so filled with passion. He made my knees go weak, and I had to hold on to Mark to keep from falling to the ground. After Mark's sweet kiss, he whispered "Good night" again. We hated to separate at night, and we were looking forward to the night that we wouldn't have to leave each other.

Chapter 5

As promised, on Monday, Dad came into the house after doing his morning feeding and cleaning out stalls. "I am going to take a shower, and then we can go car shopping if you still would like to go."

I was so excited I could hardly believe this was happening. I looked at Dad with a big smile and said, "I would love to go car shopping with you. I have $500 to put toward the car, or I can use my money to pay for the insurance and the transfer of the title. I will also need money for gas. Do you have any idea how much insurance will be?"

"I think it will cost about $250 for six months. You maybe can pay monthly if that is easier," Dad told me. We talked all the way into town and were soon driving into the car dealership.

I was so proud to walk beside my dad as the salesman showed us several good cars that we liked. I didn't know which one was the better deal. I turned to Dad and told him, "Why don't you decide on the one that you feel is the best deal. I would like you to get the best car for your money, and you are a better judge of cars than I am. I will be satisfied with any of them."

Dad seemed to appreciate the confidence I had in him, because he was beaming. We test-drove four different cars. One car had some kind of noise that Dad didn't like, so we dismissed that one. Dad said, "I like how this Camry sounds and handles. The mileage is fairly low for a 2012. If it is okay with you, let's see what kind of deal they will make on this one."

Dad was satisfied with the deal the salesman gave us. They asked for $500 down, and the rest we could finance through the Ford Credit Company. The payments were going to be $230 a month. We signed the agreement, and I hugged Dad and thanked him for helping me get car. I was so happy. Dad was beaming from ear to ear and said, "Why don't we go out to lunch. After all, it's not every day my girl gets her very own car."

Dad seemed as excited as I was at buying the car, so I said, "Lunch sounds great. Where do you want to go?"

"Why don't we go to Hardee's for a quick lunch? I have a customer coming at two o'clock, and that gives us an hour for lunch and fifteen minutes to drive home. This was fun, spending the morning with you. Did you enjoy it?" Dad asked almost reluctantly.

"Yes, Dad, I enjoyed our time together. I hope you aren't too far behind on your barn chores now. Thank you for the car again. It was nice of you to help me buy it," I said, looking and feeling like his little girl for the first time in a very long time.

Feeling very happy at the way the car buying had turned out, I followed Dad to Hardee's. It felt really good to have something of my own, even if it wasn't paid for yet.

After ordering and getting our food, we sat down in a booth. "Dad, I can't tell you how much I appreciate your help today. I'm not very knowledgeable in cars and which one is a better deal, so thank you very much. I have to find a job to make these payments. I will pay you back the $500 even if it's $50 a month. I will do what I can, depending on the job I can get. Mark felt bad that he couldn't be here to help me get a car, but I told him my dad is going to help me." Dad was actually paying attention to me after all these years, and it felt real good. I had really missed having my father be a dad.

Chapter 6

Feeling full of joy and love for the first time in a long time, I was eager to get up and get ready to go job hunting. I was anxious to drive my new car around town. It felt really good to have a set of wheels of my very own.

I stopped at the college to see if they were hiring some help to prepare for the next school year. I told them I would be a student in the fall and that I was looking for a summer job and maybe something to extend into the school year. I was taken to talk to the person who did the hiring. We talked for a few minutes, and she said they needed help in the bookstore. There were a lot of supplies coming in, and they could use help stocking the shelves. The pay was only $12 per hour, but it was a job. I would be working forty hours a week for a while. I would be able to make my car payments and then some. I told Mrs. Murphy that I would gladly take the job.

Mrs. Murphy said, "You can start tomorrow if you are free to start this soon. We pay every two weeks, and you get a lunch in the cafeteria. The variety isn't as big as when school is in full session, but there are a few summer classes going on. I will have your badge ready for you in the morning when you arrive."

"Thank you for offering me a chance to work here. I am so anxious for my classes to start in the fall. Do you think I will be able to work in the bookstore in the fall too?" I asked as we walked to the bookstore. She was going to show me around and introduce me to the gentleman in charge of the bookstore.

"If you do a good job, I don't see why you can't work all year long," Mrs. Murphy told me.

I was so excited at getting a job so soon. Mark was going to be very surprised at my good luck. I drove home feeling like the luckiest girl in Des Moines to call Mark and tell him about my great day.

The next morning, I got up and got ready to start my new job. I still couldn't believe I had a job. Just a few days ago, I was in high school and didn't know what my future held. I drove to the college and went in to start my job. I would be working with another girl who would be attending the college in the fall for her second year of classes. Carmen is a very funny girl and makes the job seem like nothing. She has worked in the bookstore since last summer. We laughed and had lunch together every day. I loved working in the bookstore and looked forward to going to work each day.

The days went by fast. Soon, I had worked two weeks, and I was given my first paycheck. I was so proud when I went to the bank to cash it. I had more money than I had ever had. I went to Kmart to buy my dad a gift. He needed a new hat. The one he was wearing was so old and dirty. I shouldn't spend my money foolishly, but I wanted to do something for my dad.

When Dad came into the house for some supper, I handed him $500. Dad looked at me in shock at getting the down payment for the car and said, "You don't have to pay me back right away. You must have gotten your first check. Do you have money for gas for the next two weeks?"

I nodded and said, "I just appreciate you lending me the money to get my first car. I really hadn't needed one until now. Thank you." Dad and I hugged, and I told him supper was ready. "Mom called and is going to be late tonight and that we should eat whenever we wanted to." Dad and I sat down at the table, and he saw the present sitting beside his place.

"What is this?" he asked, looking questionably at me.

"Oh, it's just a little something I picked up for you at the store to say 'thank you' and to say 'I love you,'" I said.

"You do know it's not necessary to buy me presents, don't you?" Dad said as he opened the gift. "A new cap! Now I can throw my dirty old one away. I just hadn't gotten around to buying one. Thank you! I love it!" Dad said as he put it on his head.

About once a week, Dad asked me to go horseback riding, go to a movie, or just go for a walk. I was getting more and more comfortable doing things with my dad.

With the end of August upon me, it was time to go to orientation at the college. I was very proud to tell the college that I didn't need financial help after all and could pay for my classes and books on my own. I didn't tell them that it was because I had a great father after all. I had never been so excited for school. The bookstore was really busy, with all the students getting their books for their classes. In no time, the shelves were getting bare. Carmen and I worked very hard to restock the shelves for the latecomers and with ongoing supplies college kids needed throughout the year.

Classes were wonderful! It made a difference to study something I was really interested in. I made the dean's list the first semester. I was ecstatic! The classes were easier than I thought they would be. I was in school from eight o'clock to two o'clock Monday through Friday. I worked from two o'clock to five o'clock to restock the books and supplies that students had bought. From the school, I would go home and make supper, clean up, then head for the library to use a computer. Dad had just gotten one, but I didn't want to try to use his because in the evenings, he would use his computer for his business. With our relationship on the mend, I didn't want to rock the boat and make unnecessary demands from my dad.

Chapter 7

By the middle of December, I was ready for a couple of weeks off school. Also, Mark would be home for the holidays. I couldn't wait to see him. I would wait for him to go shopping with me for presents for his parents, my parents, and Amy and Phil. We couldn't afford much, but it's the thought that counts. I had worked part-time at the college since the school year had started, but a lot of the money went to books and gas. I had saved $800 since I had started in June.

Amy called on Saturday morning before Mark was due home and wanted to go Christmas shopping together to get gifts for Phil and Mark. "It is really nice to spend some time together. We don't see enough of each other since we are both in college," Amy said when she picked me up at my house. Amy was attending another college in Des Moines, studying social services. We had a lovely day together, shopping and having lunch together.

Finally, on Friday night before Christmas, Mark got home even though it was snowing and blowing really bad. "It was slowgoing, but Steve and I were very careful. We wanted to get home so bad. I couldn't wait to see you, sweetie." Mark hugged and kissed me for a long time. "Shall we meet tomorrow to go Christmas shopping, or do you want to wait until Monday?"

I said, "Why don't we wait until Monday. I think the stores will be less crowded. We have a few days before Christmas."

"Okay, that's good. I might sleep until noon tomorrow. I have been up nights studying for our finals before Christmas break. How about we watch a movie tonight with the weather so bad? I might fall asleep though." Mark sounded so tired.

Monday, Mark and I went Christmas shopping at the mall. We had great success in finding inexpensive gifts for everyone. We even got little gifts for eight grandparents who were going to be at our homes for Christmas. I hadn't seen my grandparents for about five years. I hoped the weather would calm down so they could come. We went out to lunch in between hours of shopping. I had so much fun shopping with Mark. In fact, I hadn't gone shopping until I graduated from high school, and I didn't know what it was like to have fun shopping. Maybe I was having so much fun because Mark was at my side, holding my hand as we went up and down aisles.

Friday was Christmas Eve, and as we did every year, we got ready to attend candlelight services at nine o'clock. It was always such a magical service. It was like the birth of Jesus all over again. I loved singing all the Christmas hymns that we sang every Christmas season. We had bars and coffee in the fellowship hall after the service. Everyone brought some kind of bar or cake. What a wonderful time of the year! It was always my favorite.

Saturday brought a bright, sunny day with a little wind but no snow. We were up early to start Christmas dinner. We would all meet at Mark's house at noon. They had a great big dining room and always invited the Macollin family over to celebrate with them. The Macollins and Johnsons had been friends and neighbors for years. Mom and Joy were in some of the same clubs and ladies' group at church. Dad and Paul played golf and helped each other on their farms.

Mom and I had several dishes to make for the meal, so we got started early so we could be ready to leave by twelve o'clock.

Mom seemed very joyful this morning, so I thought I would take a chance to start a mother and daughter conversation with her. I asked her, "What are we going to make this year, and what do you want me to make?"

Mom smiled at me and said, "Joy and I got together to plan the menu. We are to bring the green bean casserole, a Jell-O salad, buns and five pies, pumpkin bars, and two cakes. I know it sounds like a lot of dessert, but we need some for supper too. Also, I made up some hot cocoa mix with the powdered milk, cocoa, and powdered sugar. We will need that for after the hayride. I also bought a couple bottles of wine to take."

That was more than Mom had said to me in a long time, and last time it was just to tell me to do something or ask me why something wasn't done. "Are Grandma and Grandpa coming?" I asked, hoping to keep the conversation going.

"Grandma and Grandpa Macollin are coming soon, and Grandma and Grandpa Sampson won't be here until noon. What would you like to make on the list? The pies are baked or thawed. The ingredients are on the counter for the two salads except the whipped cream and milk." Mom seemed like she was actually enjoying Christmas this year.

"I will make the salads. Do you have the recipes out for them?" I asked Mom. I had never felt so relaxed in the kitchen with Mom before. This was nice.

Grandma and Grandpa Macollin arrived, and the food was ready to go. Everyone seemed very excited for Christmas this year. Gifts were packed in my car and the food in Mom and Dad's. After Grandma and Grandpa Sampson arrived, we all drove over to Paul and Joy Johnson's home.

Dinner was fabulous. The table was decorated very festive, and everyone was dressed so nice. Each family had brought some dishes to contribute to the meal. What a wonderful day we were having. Everyone was so full they couldn't move. We sat and talked for about an hour to let our dinner settle while we drank coffee and wine. It was wonderful to visit with the grandmas and grandpas. I hadn't seen them for so long, and they were excited about my courses I was taking at the community college. They agreed that the medical field was a safe field to be in.

Finally, we had to get up to put the food away and clean up. It didn't take long since there were four grandmothers, Joy, Mom, Amy, April, Sue, and myself. We were constantly bumping into one another. We all laughed about it, and Grandma Macollin said we had too many cooks in the kitchen. She said it was an old saying that her mother had used. Great-grandma never wanted anyone else in the kitchen when she was cooking a meal.

At three o'clock, we decided to exchange gifts. I had never received so many gifts in my life. I think I had ten gifts when it was my turn to open mine. We took turns opening our gifts so we could actually see what everyone got. I was about to open a small box that felt very light, and I couldn't figure out what it could be. Inside, there was a gift card, and Dad said to read the card out loud. "My gift to you is a four-year-old palomino mare that needs someone to love her. She was an abused horse at a farm that couldn't take care of her. She is very sweet, and I hope you will love her and care for her."

"Oh my! A horse for me! This is so wonderful. I can't wait to see her. Thank you so much!"

Dad had gotten three horses from the farm that had abused animals a month or so ago. "These poor horses were about starved and would not have lasted through the winter if someone didn't give them the love and care they needed to survive. The sheriff had come and asked if I could take on three more horses and nurse them back to health and then maybe find homes for them. I really like this one little mare. I thought we might keep her. She has a wonderful disposition and is coming along nicely." Dad sounded very excited about the horses as he explained about acquiring a horse for me.

Everyone enjoyed their gifts, and then we decided to bundle up and go on a hayride. It was a nice, crisp evening, and we sang Christmas carols to our heart's content. Mark brought his guitar to accompany us. We rode for two hours, and we were just beginning to get cold, so we headed for home to enjoy hot cocoa and some ham sandwiches, salads, and desserts. What a wonderful hayride this had been.

We ate a light supper of leftovers and hot cocoa or wine. Everyone was so joyful they didn't want the evening to end. Finally, at eight o'clock, everyone left after wishing everyone else a Merry Christmas.

The day after Christmas, I dressed in blue jeans and a sweatshirt to go out to the barn to see my new horse. I was so excited to see her. Dad was just feeding her when I opened the barn door.

"You're just in time to see this young lady," Dad told me as I approached the stall.

I looked in to see the horse, and she looked at me with the biggest loveable eyes I had ever seen. She whinnied at me, as if saying "Good morning" to me. With a smile on my face, I entered her stall, and my heart went out to her. She was the prettiest horse I had ever seen even though she still had some sores that were healing on her face, legs, and chest. She had gained some weight thanks to the extra nutritional food Dad had been feeding her. I put out my hand for her to sniff. I rubbed my hand over her face and shoulders, and she leaned into me with her head.

"Dad, I love her. I think we will be best friends. Can we ride her, or does she have to be trained?" I hugged her for several minutes. "Does she have a name?"

"I don't know what her name was. We will have to rename her because unfortunately, she can't tell us what it was. You can rename her," Dad told me.

"I think I will name her Hope. There is hope for her now with someone to love her." I felt Hope and I had something in common. Dad finally showed me some love that I desperately needed, and Hope finally had someone to love her.

"I think I will give her another month to heal and gain her strength. Then we will put a saddle on her and see what she does. You want to be out here when I saddle her? I can let you know so you can be here. In the meantime, you can brush her and lead her around. Just spending time with her will help her," Dad said very thoughtfully.

"I would like to be here to see how she reacts to a saddle. I have a feeling she is going to work out just fine," I said, brushing my hand over her nose before letting her finish her breakfast. "I love you," I said to Hope.

Finally, about a month later, Dad asked me if I was ready to saddle up Hope. This was so exciting! I had gone out and led her around and talked to her quite often since Christmas. She was so willing to do what I asked of her.

I hurriedly ate my breakfast and went out to the barn with Dad.

"Why don't you go and get her from her stall. I'll get a bridle and saddle for her," Dad told me very calmly. He was so good working with horses because he was so calm himself.

I brushed Hope until her coat shined. Then we put on her blanket and saddle and finally a bridle. She took to it like she was saddled every day.

Dad took her out into the arena and got into the saddle. Hope just stood there, waiting for a command. Dad told her to walk, and she did. Then they trotted and finally cantered. She rode like a dream. "Do you want to give her a try? She seems very calm. Be easy with her mouth," Dad told me.

With a smile on my face, I climbed into the saddle. She was so calm I thought I was riding a well-trained old mare. "Dad, I love her. Thank you for giving her to me. I will love her forever!"

I rode her for about thirty minutes and decided we shouldn't tire her too much as she wasn't used to a lot of exercise. I took off her saddle and bridle and brushed her well. I loved spending time with my very own horse. I led her into her stall and gave her some hay to munch on. I kissed her on the nose and left the barn.

Outside in the crisp winter air, I walked on the shoveled trail to the house. I felt like skipping, but the path was slippery from some rain we had had the night before, so I walked to the house feeling the joy of saving this horse. Yes, this friendship was going to work out just fine. We had both found the love we needed.

Chapter 8

Soon the year was drawing to an end, and I had to decide where to take my clinicals. Our instructor told us, "The clinics in Des Moines are very helpful in letting our assistants do their clinicals there."

"I will start with Riverside Clinic and see if I can take my clinicals there. I think I would feel very comfortable there as I have been a patient there since birth, and I know the staff. They are wonderful." I had to stop talking to myself, but it's easier for me to decide if I talked out loud.

Des Moines had four clinics. Riverside Clinic, the clinic I went to, was operated by Dr. Wells, a longtime friend and doctor of the Macollins and Johnsons. Dr. Wells and his wife, Michelle, had lived in Des Moines all their lives. Michelle was Dr. Wells's assistant and had told me at a visit she wanted to continue her artwork and maybe do some volunteer work for the community. Michelle wanted to fulfill her dreams before she was too old to enjoy them. She wanted to have more time to paint than she had, because working at the clinic five days a week didn't give her much extra time. The local art gallery held some of her work but was asking for more, for a bigger assortment for the buyers who were local and outside the community.

I called and asked if I could come in to talk to Dr. Wells about doing my clinicals at their clinic. I hoped I sounded like a mature person ready to take on the world, even though I was very scared to get out in the big, wide world. I knew the clinic helped in training the graduating assistants, as I had seen them at the clinic before.

I was told to come in that afternoon to talk to Dr. Wells. *That was quick,* I thought somewhat reluctantly. Maybe it would be a flat *no*, because that was how my whole life had been. Not many people ever wanted to help me out. The exception being Mark and his family. "Am I overreacting? Okay, well, I can do this."

I rummaged through her closet for something that looked businesslike and flattering, hopefully not boring. My clothes selection was very slim. I settled on a brown skirt and a cream-colored silk blouse I had splurged on during the summer. Even though the outfit had cost more than I had ever spent on clothes before, I had hoped the outfit would come in handy someday. *What better occasion to wear it than this?* I thought.

After styling my hair and doing my makeup, I was headed for the door. My palms were wet with nervous moisture. "Calm down," I told myself. "You know Dr. Wells, and he has been a friend to you since you were born. If you don't get to finish your training at the Riverside Clinic, you can go to another clinic." With that, I grabbed my car keys and headed to my car. I had to concentrate on my driving, but it was hard as nervous as I was. Finally, I pulled into the clinic parking lot. I said a little prayer before getting out of my car, straightened my shoulders, and headed for the door with a smile on my face.

Dr. Wells happened to be at the front desk when I walked in. He smiled and motioned for me to follow him. "Come in, come in, Katie. How are you?" Dr. Wells asked as he ushered me down the hall into his office. Dr. Wells had always been a wonderful man—honest, fair, and loyal to the core. He was like the friend and mentor everyone looked up to.

"Let's go in here so we can talk where it is quiet," Dr. Wells said with a big friendly smile on his face. He put his hand on my back to steer me into his office. He told me to take a seat across from his desk. I looked around, feeling very nervous. I hoped I didn't appear too nervous even though I was sweating bullets and felt like I was going to hyperventilate. *Oh well, I guess I'm in the right place if I pass out.*

I was so nervous. *Why am I so nervous? I have known Dr. Wells all my life. Calm down. I just have to ask if I can do my clinicals here. You can do this!* With that, I took a deep breath and tried to relax.

"Well, I hear you just need to do your clinicals to complete your medical assistant training. Is that right?" Dr. Wells was always ready to help the young men and women with further training. He had done it for years.

I smiled and tried to appear relaxed. "Dr. Wells, I am ready to do my clinicals, and I was wondering if you would let me do them here." *There, I have done it, and I feel more relaxed now. I can't believe I talked so fast. I'm sure he knows I'm very nervous.* I was so afraid of the answer I didn't want to hear it.

"Congratulations on accomplishing your educational goals. I would be very happy to have you do your clinicals here. You have grown into a fine young woman. I remember all the times I treated that little girl with the big brown eyes and cute little smile. What happened to her? You certainly have grown into a beautiful young woman," Dr. Wells happily commented with a big smile on his face.

I couldn't believe I had heard Dr. Wells right. *Did he say I could do my clinicals here?*

"When will you be able to start?" Dr. Wells asked.

"I can start next Monday, if that's all right?" I exclaimed with great excitement.

"I had heard that you were taking the medical assistant training and was hoping you would come here for your clinicals. Actually, if you would be interested in a full-time job after graduation, I think I have a position open for you, if you would like it. As you know, my wife has been assisting me here at the clinic for a while now, and she wants to pursue her art career and maybe do some volunteer work for the community. I just haven't made a move yet. She doesn't forget to remind me every once in a while, so this just might be the right time. I will talk to her and see if she still wants out of here. Hopefully, I will have an answer for you in the next week or so."

"Thank you very much for letting me do my clinicals here, and I would love to work full-time for you. I think I can be a great asset to this office." I couldn't have been happier at the chance to have a full-time job at the clinic. That seemed too easy. I thought I would have to go through a lot of interviews and still maybe not get a job. That was just too easy.

CHAPTER 9

I left the doctor's office walking on cloud nine. Pulling out my cell phone, I dialed Mark's number on speed dial. "I can't wait to tell him. He will never believe I might have a job already." I was talking to myself again. I hoped no one heard or saw me, for heaven's sake. The phone rang and rang, but there was no answer. He was probably in class or at the library. Disappointed, I called Amy, Mark's sister and my best friend in the whole world. I had to tell somebody about my news before I burst.

Amy and I have been close friends and neighbors forever. Amy was like the sister that I never had. We hung out a lot in school and shared our deepest secrets. Amy lent me clothes or whatever I needed. We were the same size, so that made sharing easy. She is the kind of friend every girl would love to have. I counted my blessings every day that I have her in my corner, and I felt very lucky!

Amy answered on the first ring, sounding a little out of breath. "Hi, Katie. What's up?"

"Amy, you will never guess what just happened to me! You will never ever guess!" I was rambling on, and I couldn't help myself. Good things didn't usually happen to me.

"What?" Amy had no idea what had me so excited. "You will have to tell me because I have no idea. I'm at the mall and just finished my shopping. Mom wanted me to pick up a few things for her. Do you want to meet me here for coffee so you can tell me your good news, as it seems you're about to burst with excitement?" Amy wanted to share in my good news, as good friends do.

Ten minutes later I was pulling into a parking spot. A couple of cars over, Amy was just putting her purchases into her car. She looked up, saw me, and started to wave and yell out to me. We practically ran to each other and hugged and laughed until we were both breathless. Then we headed to the restaurant in the mall, talking and laughing all the while.

After ordering our lattes, Amy anxiously asked me about my news. Amy saw that I was really beaming and hadn't seen me this happy in a very long time. "What is your big news?"

"I just talked to Dr. Wells about my clinicals, and he said I could do them at his clinic. Then he asked if I would like a full-time job at the clinic. I guess Michelle wants to quit to paint for the art gallery. Can you believe it?" I explained, being so filled with excitement I could hardly sit still. "The clinic is also hiring two more doctors, so Dr. Wells doesn't have to work so hard. He has been lost since Dr. Wright passed away of pancreatic cancer. There will be a Dr. Steve Killen and a Dr. Mark Evans. Your brother and Steve are friends. They played baseball in high school, and he is attending Iowa State University too. You remember him, don't you, Amy? He is a wonderful man. Dr. Evans is a pediatrician and will therefore handle most, if not all the pregnancies and baby checkups. That should really help out with Dr. Wells's patient load. Dr. Evans's wife, Angie, is a lab technician and will also be working for the clinic. They still have to hire another receptionist and another lab technician to help with the growing clinic."

"This is wonderful!" Amy was very excited to share in her friend's good fortune. "I think this calls for a celebration. Let's order hot fudge sundaes in honor of your upcoming job," Amy suggested laughingly. "Did you call Mark? He will want to know right away."

"I don't know if I actually have the job yet, but Dr. Wells sounded very sure Michelle would quit the clinic if they could hire a replacement. I tried to call Mark, but he didn't answer. I will try later. He will be happy to know I might be working and saving money for the wedding. Sorry, I didn't mean for you to be second on my sharing list, but I am very, very fond of your brother," I exclaimed. "One of us needs to work as he is still in college. We need to find a house and furnish it. That takes a lot of money."

"I know you will enjoy working for Dr. Wells. He is an amazing man. I can't believe you found a job so easily, I hope I can. I am so happy for you. You deserve this, and it's about time your life took a turn in the right direction." Amy sounded almost as excited as I was, and I knew Amy missed having a sister as much as I did. "I know Mark will get a job as soon as he graduates, Katie. He will have to pass the bar, but I'm sure he will do that with flying colors. Then he will have to find a job. My dad said if Mark couldn't find a job right away, he would hire him on for a year or so, just to get him going. It was nice of Dad to offer, but I don't think Mark will have a problem joining another firm. There are several in Des Moines.'

"What if, and I mean if, he can't find a job here?" I murmured in a low, nervous tone. "If he doesn't have a job, we won't be able to get married. My parents won't pay for the wedding. I really need to talk to Mark. My stomach hurts just thinking about postponing the wedding. I've been looking forward to this wedding for several years, and I can't wait any longer."

"I think Mark will do everything possible to make this all come true because he loves you and always has. He's good at whatever he does, and he won't let you down." Amy could always comfort me with her calming voice.

"Thank you, Amy, you're the best! I don't know what I would do if I didn't have you to keep me grounded," I told Amy with a half smile. It was nice having Amy to talk to.

I sighed and looked out the restaurant window, wishing Mark was done with school too so we could get married and start our lives together. Unfortunately, he had six very long months of school left.

"How is your job hunting coming?" I asked. Amy was doing her year of training to be a full-fledged accountant. She had about two months left and was out looking for her first job.

"I have applied at the Ford car dealership, and Southern Memorial Hospital is also hiring. I have had an interview with the hospital, and that sounds good, but I want to interview for the car dealership also. Then I can decide which sounds the best." Amy sounded anxious to start her first real job also.

"They both sound like they would be very fulfilling jobs, Amy. Are the benefits similar?" I asked, hoping to be as helpful to Amy as Amy had been for me.

"The hospital has a little better benefits with a 401k plan that the car dealership doesn't. That's the main difference. The wage is almost the same. The hospital is a dollar more per hour, and the hours are better," Amy informed me.

"I would say the hospital sounds like a winner, but the decision has to be yours. Have you talked it over with Phil yet?" I said thoughtfully. Phil is Amy's fiancé, and they were planning their wedding for July, which was right around the corner. He graduated a year before Amy and is part of an architectural firm in Des Moines. They are a very lovely couple, and Phil would support Amy any way he could.

"I will be seeing Phil later tonight, so we will discuss my job options then. Well, I better get going, Katie. I promised Mom I would start supper for her, because she had a meeting after work today. Why don't you come have supper at my house tonight? We can make supper together, and you can share your good news with Mom and Dad. They would love to hear it."

I looked at Amy longingly. "You are so lucky to have such loving parents, and they are lucky to have wonderful children like you and Mark. I would give anything to have a family like yours. Your parents have always been so good to me, and I love them like my own parents."

Amy looked longingly at me and said, "Your mom and dad have started to see you for the wonderful person you are. They are talking to you, and your dad is doing a few things with you. Soon, you will have a family of your own. Once you and Mark are husband and wife, you can build a loving family all your own."

I liked the sound of that. I reached over and took Amy's hand and gave it a squeeze. "I would love to have supper with you and your parents. I don't know how you always seem to make me see the better things in life. You should be a psychologist instead of an accountant. I love you!"

Amy and I left a tip and exited our booth. After paying for our sundaes and lattes, we walked out of the restaurant, laughing and acting like high school girls. I was glad I had Amy to share everything with. We said we would see each other at Amy's house, and I followed Amy to her house.

While supper was cooking, I went out on the patio to try to call Mark again. I had to tell him my good fortune. The phone rang three times before Mark picked up.

"Hi, sweetheart. How is my favorite girl in the whole world?" Mark gleefully expressed.

"Hi right back to you, sweetie!" I said dreamily. My heart always sped up when I talked to Mark. Love was in the air. "I just wanted to fill you in on the best day I have had since I saw you last. I am able to do my clinicals at Dr. Wells's clinic, and he said he would hire me on if I wanted to work for him. He has to talk to Michelle to see if she still wants to quit the clinic and pursue her art career, but he sounded hopeful. They are also hiring two more doctors, so they need two more assistants. Isn't that wonderful?"

"Yes, that is wonderful news! I figured Dr. Wells would let you work there. I know you will be a good assistant. I talked to Steve last week, and he seemed hopeful that Dr. Wells would allow him to join the staff there as well. Steve will be replacing Dr. Wright. He wants to be close to his family, and I don't blame him. I would not want to move away from Des Moines in order to find a job," Mark said and didn't seem surprised that Steve had applied at the clinic.

Mark and I talked for a few more minutes and said our good-byes. We were so in love it was hard to say good-bye. With tears in my eyes, I returned inside the house to set the table for supper.

Mark's parents were very happy when they heard my good news. "It's a good thing we had Amy pick up some pie today so we can have pie and ice cream to celebrate." Paul hugged me, and when he put me back on my feet, he had a twinkle in his eyes. I love Mark's parents so much and envied Amy and Mark. Oh, to have such loving parents!

Chapter 10

Monday morning, I was up early to start my clinicals at Riverside Clinic. I was so excited I didn't know I could eat any breakfast but felt I needed something. Munching on a piece of toast, I went over everything I had learned. Getting everything right would go a long way to assure Dr. Wells that I knew my stuff.

I took a deep breath as I entered the clinic. Right behind me, Sarah, a girl from my class, was entering the clinic too. We said hi, and smiling, we walked in together. That made us both feel better about starting this new journey. Angie Tollefson, who was the receptionist, welcomed us with a big smile and a hug. "Welcome, Katie, I will show you where Michelle is." Angie led me down the hall toward Dr. Wells's office. Evidently, Michelle, Dr. Wells's wife of twenty-two years, was in his office. They both welcomed me with hugs, and we decided to get the day started.

Returning to the front desk, Angie went to Sarah and said, "Sarah, I will introduce you to Dr. Evans. He is new too. He is just starting today too. Carol has been with our clinic for a few years and is pregnant. She will be going on maternity leave in a couple of weeks, and she will help you learn the job."

I worked alongside Michelle and was flying high with enthusiasm as we roomed patient after patient. I didn't know if I would ever be as fast as Michelle was. When we had a few minutes between patients, Michelle and I were talking. "You are very good at this job. Are you sure you haven't done this before? I feel like you are training me. That school has certainly stepped up their program. It used to be, when assistants graduated, we would have to spend a lot of time training them, and I wondered what they spent their time doing at that college. You are a natural!"

"Thank you, I am really enjoying this work. You have a nice, easy flow to your clinic. I am very pleased that you approve of my performance. I hope I will get faster," I expressed to Michelle.

Michelle assured me that I would feel more comfortable as time went on and that I was doing very well.

Between patients, I asked Sarah if she liked working here. She seemed a little overwhelmed but said she liked it. "I think I will get used to it. Carol is a very patient and a good teacher. She makes me feel very comfortable," Sarah said.

At twelve o'clock, Dr. Wells announced that we were all going to lunch together to celebrate the start of the new assistants and Dr. Evans. Dr. Wells and his wife were so generous and always made everyone feel like they were special. *I think this is going to work out very well,* I thought to myself. *I already feel at home.*

When I got home at five thirty, I quickly dialed Mark's number. He answered on the second ring. "Hello, Katie," Mark answered. "How was your first day of clinicals? Did they have to fire you on your first day?" I knew he was teasing like he often did.

"Mark, you don't get fired when you do clinicals. You might get yelled at if you aren't doing your job, but not fired," I murmured with a sigh. "I had a wonderful day! Dr. Wells and Michelle are wonderful people. They are easy to work with. Sarah, a girl from my class, is working with Dr. Evans. It was nice that I wasn't the only new person starting today. I think I will accept the job Dr. Wells offered me if Michelle wants to quit. I almost hope she does. Does that make me a bad person?"

"Not at all. Dr Wells offered you the job knowing Michelle wants out," Mark offered in support of me. "I don't think you could find a better clinic to work at. We know Dr. Wells and Michelle are wonderful people, and Steve will be there soon. You will like him too."

"I just had to share my day with you. I hope I didn't take you away from something important," I said reluctantly. "I miss you so much and wish you were here with me. I love you!"

"I love you too, sweetie. You never have to worry about taking me away from something. If I'm at the library, I don't usually answer my phone, but you caught me at a good time. I know it's hard on you with me not home to talk to every day. It won't be for much longer. Hang in there, okay?"

I murmured a sigh and said I would try to be patient. I didn't want to make it any harder on Mark than it was because I knew it has been hard on him being away too, so I didn't express my frustration any more than I already had. The last thing he needed was a nagging fiancée.

On Friday, Dr. Wells asked to see me in his office right after lunch. *Oh no, did I do something wrong?* My heart was beating so fast I thought I might need medical attention. Shyly I slipped into the office and stood in front of Dr. Wells's desk and probably looked a little pale, because Dr. Wells told me to sit down and relax. I sat, prepared for the worst.

"Katie, Michelle tells me you are doing absolutely marvelous as an assistant. I am very happy to hear this as I would like to offer you that full-time job we talked about. Michelle was thrilled when I told her I would like to hire you to replace her. You will make my wife a very happy woman if you accept this job," Dr. Wells told me with a big smile on his face. "I think you and I can work very good together. What do you think? Are you willing to give it a try?"

"Oh, Dr. Wells, you don't know how happy I am to hear this. I would love to accept this position. I thought I had done something wrong and I was going to be reprimanded for it. This is a dream come true! I know shouldn't say this as it is not very professional, but I love you and Michelle. You have always been someone I could go to when things were getting out of control as I was growing up. You knew when I was thirteen and couldn't handle my problems at home and school, you got me help. I can't thank you enough for this. I will not let you down. I'm rambling, aren't I? I'm sorry, I do that when I'm excited. I will get back to work now. Thank you very much."

Dr. Wells stood, came around his desk, and pulled me into a hug. "That's probably not very professional either, but you know what, I don't care. You have always held a special piece of my heart, and I want to be the one that gives you a comfortable position in the workforce. Being your doctor all these years has given us a special relationship. That is only natural. I know you will do well. I have nothing but good reports about you. Let's go see some patients, shall we?"

I left the office at the close of the day, walking on air. *This just couldn't be happening, could it? But I think it is. It's going to take a while to sink in.*

Chapter 11

On Friday night, graduation from Riverside Community College was taking place at the auditorium. I hadn't invited anyone since Mark said it would make it real tight to try to get home as his last class ended at five o'clock. It was a two-hour drive without heavy traffic. I told him it was all right; it wasn't a big deal. Getting my diploma was all that mattered, and he could see that when he came home. I suppose his parents would come if I had told them, but I didn't want to take up their Friday night sitting in a hot auditorium, listening to long speeches and a long list of graduates' names read off as they received their diplomas. Amy knew, but she said she had plans. I had told my dad when graduation was, but I hadn't heard if he was coming. Oh well, it was all right. I would get my diploma and go home to celebrate by myself. I would be all right.

Graduation was long and hot. I got my diploma and was relieved when it was over. I went to the room where we were to return my gown and headed for my car. All of a sudden, I heard someone yelling behind me. I turned around, and Mark's parents, Amy, Phil, and Mark were coming toward me. Right behind them were Mom and Dad. We all hugged, and they congratulated me. What in the world! I hadn't invited them, but I was really glad that they all cared enough to come.

Mark was the last one to come up to me, and he drew me into his arms and kissed me. My head went light, and I was speechless. After I could count on my voice to say something, I asked what they were all doing here.

"You didn't think we were going to let you graduate without us seeing it, did you?" Mark asked.

"How did you get home on time for the ceremony? It's a long drive. You couldn't have made it in two hours. Your last class doesn't get out until five o'clock," I asked, still not believing they were all here.

"I'm bad, but I skipped my last class so I could leave at three o'clock. This is important to you, so it is important to me. I wanted to be here to share in your accomplishment. I'm very proud of you!" Mark smiled, looking into my eyes, and kissed me and hugged me again. Finally, he said, "Let's go home."

Mark wanted me to drive to my house and drop my car off and then go back to his house with him. I was glad I didn't have to go home alone. I was so happy I could spend the weekend with Mark. Mark came around the car to open my door and took my hand in his to escort me to the house. Mark said he wanted to talk to me alone for a minute, so we went into the living room. After about twenty minutes, Mark suggested we go out to the patio. As we stepped outside, there were several people on the patio. "Surprise!" they all shouted. I could not believe this.

"You did this for me? Thank you, I am so shocked! Thank you all for coming," I told the group of friends and family members. Dr. Wells; Michelle; Jeff and his wife, April; Dan and his girlfriend, Lori; Amy; Phil; Mark's mom and dad; Angie and Lisa from the office; Dr. Kilen and his wife, Sara; and Dr. Evans and his wife, Angie, were all there. "This is fantastic!"

Wine was passed out, and they toasted me. I felt like a queen. Mark gave a speech about how hard I had worked to go to college and how proud he was of me for becoming a medical assistant. They had prepared a feast with a cake to honor me. The party lasted well into the night. Mark got out his guitar, and everyone did some singing. It was quite amazing.

My parents didn't stay all that long, but I was very pleased they came at all. My relationship with my dad had changed in the last year or so. The relationship with my mom was also a little better. They told me "Congratulations" and that they were proud of me. I was glad they had come. So I said, "Thank you for coming." They each gave me a hug and kiss, and I was shocked and practically in tears. First high school graduation, and now college graduation. Maybe they were coming around.

Mark must have seen what had happened, because he came over and put his arms around me and gave me a hug. As I was hugging him, I whispered, "Thank you, I love you." I was a little sad to see them go, but there were lots of other guests still there to party. People had brought gifts and cards. The gift I was touched by the most was a new stethoscope from Dr. Wells and Michelle. I had been using one of Michelle's until I could buy one of my own. All in all, it turned out to be a pretty good night, thanks to Mark, his parents, my parents, and my friends.

Chapter 12

It was amazing as we went over the small hill and as the campus came into view. I had never seen a college as big and beautiful as the campus of Iowa State. I had attended college, but I could only go to the community college in Des Moines. The money just wasn't there for me to attend a major college. Anyway, I wanted to be a medical assistant, and I could get that training at the community college.

I had graduated and now worked at one of the four medical clinics in Des Moines. I had been hired right out of school after doing clinical training. It helped that the head doctor was our family physician. Dr. Wells was a great doctor, very caring and gentle. I loved working for him.

We finally pulled into a parking space near the auditorium at the college where Mark, my fiancé, had been attending college for the past four years, pursuing a career in law. He had been going to school year-round to graduate early. I was so proud of him. He had worked really hard, cramming five years into four years so we could get married when he graduated.

Mark's parents, Paul and Joy Johnson, asked me to attend the graduation ceremony with them. Amy, Mark's sister, Phil, Amy's fiancé, and I were sitting in the backseat. I was so happy they had invited me to come along. Amy seemed to be as excited as I was to see this college although she had attended another college in Des Moines, but it was not as big as this one. Amy was now an accountant, working for the Southern Medical Hospital in Des Moines.

We got out of the car and made our way to the auditorium. The auditorium was enormous, and all you could see were people everywhere. I gazed over the sea of people in the auditorium. So many people. How would I ever find Mark?

All of a sudden, somebody grabbed me from behind. I turned around to find Mark right there behind me. I gazed at him with great admiration and love. He looked so handsome in his cap and gown. Mark gathered me in his arms to kiss me. It felt so good to have his arms around me at last. It was like there was no one else in the auditorium, only us.

"You look so handsome, and I am so proud of you," I told Mark as I threw my arms around his neck. "How did you find us in all these people? There must be five thousand people here."

"I was waiting for you by the door so I could say hi before the ceremony." Mark was beaming with enthusiasm. "I have missed you so much, and I am so sorry I didn't get home the last three weekends, but I really had to cram for my finals."

"I know you had to study, Mark. I'm not upset with you for not coming home," I told him, smiling. "I just missed you, and I am really glad you will be coming home for good."

"I knew I wouldn't get much studying done if I had you to look at, which would be more pleasing to the eye, but that would not get the grades I wanted. Now I can devote all my time to you and starting my career," Mark said somewhat apologetically.

"I'm just glad this day has finally arrived so you can go home for good," I whispered in his ear as I nestled into his neck and gave him another kiss. I didn't want to let go of Mark's hands; I was squeezing them so tight Mark had to pry my hands away.

"I would love to stay with you, but I should probably get down there." Mark was about to burst with excitement. He gave me one more kiss, and then Mark left us. We made our way through the many ambling people to find some seats.

The ceremony was very sad, exciting, and solemn all at the same time. Like any graduation, the students make lasting friendships and it's sad to go their separate ways in the end. Mark had made many friends and seemed quite popular, as everybody he met had something to say or to joke about with him. I could see him laughing and chatting as he made his way out of the auditorium.

It took us some time, but we finally found seats fairly close to the front. As I looked at the program, I was so stunned and had to do a double take. Then I shrieked with excitement and leaned over to ask Mark's mom and dad if they had looked at the program. "Did you see who the valedictorian is?" I asked them. They looked twice and saw that Mark was the valedictorian. They couldn't believe what they saw either. "Mark didn't tell us. He must have wanted to surprise us. We certainly are surprised!" Joy was almost yelling to be heard above the noise in the auditorium.

At seven o'clock, the music started, and the graduates marched in and took their seats in the front of the auditorium. After the dean spoke for about twenty minutes, he announced that he was turning the ceremony over to someone else. Then he said, "I am very proud to introduce the valedictorian of 2015, Mr. Mark Johnson. Mark is one of the most amazing men I have ever had the pleasure to meet and work with in the twenty-five years of my career. He has worked very hard and has been a mentor to other law students. I have the great pleasure to give you Mr. Mark Johnson."

We all stood up and cheered as Mark took the podium to give his speech. He was a good speaker, and we were all very proud of him. At the end, the students made their way to the podium to receive their diplomas. It was such an honor to witness this ceremony.

At last, the ceremony was over, and we waited for some of the crowd to clear out. We were going to meet Mark at his house he had been sharing with four other guys for the past three years. We would help pack him up so we could all go home at long last. I would bet my last dollar that he was probably all packed up, ready to go home even though this had been his home for the last four years.

It took us about half an hour to get to the house with the traffic being so crazy. I was right. Mark was all packed up and ready to go.

"Why didn't you tell me you were the valedictorian?" I asked, slugging him in the arm. "I was shocked!" Then we hugged and laughed for a few minutes. Finally, Mark decided we better get going since we had at least a two-hour drive ahead of us.

"Let's get this stuff in the cars and be on our way." Mark sounded a little sad to be leaving but also anxious to start the next stage of his life.

"Did you leave a little room in your car for me?" I asked, hoping he had so I could ride home with him.

"I think my car is pretty full," Mark replied. Almost immediately, I saw a grin start to spread across his sexy face. I knew he was just teasing me. "Do you even have to ask? Of course I left room for my favorite girl in the whole world. That's why I had to put a few things in Mom and Dad's car. I don't ever want to be away from you ever again, my beautiful lady." Then he kissed me, and my heart did that pitter-patter it always did when Mark was near me.

I knew Mark loved me with his whole heart. We had grown up together and played together since we were infants. If someone had told me fifteen years ago that I would be engaged to be married to this handsome hunk, I would never have believed them. Yet here I am, engaged to my handsome soul mate of so many years. I was half-afraid that Mark would find someone new and better at college and I would be left with a broken heart. I wasn't the prettiest and most intellectual person in the world. He told me he wasn't at college to find a new girlfriend, but I always had my insecurities and prayed he would come back home to me. My wish had come true. There we were, going home together, or at least to the same town where we would be married in three and a half months.

The drive home was the most wonderful trip I had ever been on. Mark held my hand all the way, and I was in heaven. We talked and laughed about everything that had been going on. We hadn't seen each other for a month, and we longed to connect again.

When we were nearing home, Joy called on her cell phone. "We are going to stop for coffee and pie before we go home. Do you want to stop?" Joy asked. "We are stopping at Perkins."

"Do you want to stop?" Mark asked me, followed by a yawn. It seemed like he was very tired, but he always wanted to please me, so he let me make the decision.

"Only if you're not too tired. We don't have to stay too long. You sound quite tired. Were you up early this morning?" I was hoping Mark would stop because I didn't want the evening to end yet, also knowing that he would take me home to sleep in my own bed all alone. It felt too good being with Mark. "I am a little hungry since we had supper so early in order to leave for Iowa State."

"I am sort of hungry too, so we can stop. This has been such a special day for me, I think we should celebrate. I think Mom and Dad want to share in my achievements." Mark admitted that he was proud of his achievements and wanted to share them with his parents. They were the greatest parents any guy could have. He loved his whole family.

Mark and I pulled up at my home close to midnight. It had been a long day, filled with a lot of excitement, but neither Mark nor I made a move to get out of the car. Mark pulled me into his arms and kissed me with great passion, then deepened the kiss. After a lot of kissing and caressing, leaving both Mark and me breathless, we finally came up for air.

"Mark, I have something for your graduation. I hope you can use it in your office when you get one." I handed him a brightly wrapped gift. As he opened it, I felt like maybe it wasn't enough. He had done so much for my graduation. But as he opened it, his eyes got very large as he saw two gold picture frames, and he looked like he might cry. "I love it! I can display my diploma in one and my bar certificate in the other. Thank you very much."

"If you want a different color or if they aren't the right size, we can exchange them," I said hesitantly.

"I really like the gold, and I think the size will be good. These are perfect. How did you know I needed these?" Mark asked.

"I was at Hallmark the other day, and it was like they jumped out at me, so I bought them."

"Well, thank you. I love them!" Mark repeated.

"I suppose we should get some sleep, unfortunately in our own beds." Mark almost breathed the words, not really wanting to leave me at my house. "I can't wait until we can just go home together and hold each other in bed and make love until all hours of the night."

My parents were very firm about me being a virgin when I got married. It was very hard, but I was not going to have my father look down on me in shame. I don't know why I thought I had to please him, but I felt I should honor my father. I didn't want to do anything to harm the relationship we had built in the last year or so.

"I can't wait to be able to stay with you either," I moaned deep in my throat. "When do you want to get together to discuss the wedding? We have some things that need to be decided now. I made the decisions I could, but I would like your input in a few of these decisions."

"Do you want me to pick you up for church in the morning? Then you can have dinner at my house, and we can discuss these plans of ours," Mark willingly expressed.

"Okay, that sounds good. I look forward to seeing you in the morning," I answered very sleepily. I could hardly keep my eyes open.

"Come on, let's get you inside so you can get some sleep. If I don't leave you soon, we might both regret our actions in the morning. You know what I mean? Will you dream about me?" Mark asked with a sexy tilt of his head and dreamy blue eyes that looked hazy with desire.

"I always dream about you, my wonderful, loving man," I replied sleepily.

Mark and I slowly got out of the car, not sure our legs would support us. Mark put his arm around my shoulders as the we walked to the door. At the door, Mark turned me to face him and bent a little to kiss me good-night. "I love you, Katie, very much. Good night, princess."

"Good night, and I love you too." With that, I opened the door and went inside. I changed into pajamas, brushed my teeth, and fell into bed. It had been a wonderful day getting Mark home at last. I quickly fell asleep dreaming of the love of my life.

Chapter 13

I couldn't believe morning came so soon. It seemed like I had just gone to sleep. But thinking about being with Mark and his family all day, I got out of bed and quickly showered and decided what to wear to church.

After a quick piece of toast and coffee, I brushed my teeth and waited for Mark to show up. Mark was always prompt and drove up as I was putting on my shoes.

The church was packed by the time Mark pulled into the parking lot. It took a while to get inside since everybody we met up with stopped to talk to Mark, asking how he was and congratulating him on his graduation from college.

Pastor Bailey was waiting to enter the sanctuary but smiled a big smile as he looked up and saw Mark and me enter the church. He came toward Mark with his hand extended to welcome Mark home. They talked for a few minutes, then we went in to find a seat.

Mark's parents were seated up front, so we joined them. They were beaming with admiration of their son being home for good.

My parents were also at the service and nodded and smiled when they saw us come in to find seats. I was hoping they would beckon us over to say hi, but that never happened, much to my disappointment. There was always that doubt if they accepted me as their daughter, and I didn't know if I was imagining the distance between us or if it was real. Maybe I needed a session with Dr. Simpson to deal with these feelings.

Mark and I joined Joy and Paul in the front of the church. They were very happy to have us join them.

Pastor Bailey opened the service by welcoming everyone, and then it came. "We have a very special member joining us this morning. He will be a future lawyer of our community, as he just graduated from law school last night. I would like you to welcome Mark Johnson back home to begin his career in Des Moines." Everybody applauded, and Mark stood to acknowledge the congregation.

After church, Mark and I stood around, talking and drinking coffee with members of the church they had always attended. Everyone was happy to wish Mark well and hoped he would stay here to practice in his hometown, and I left the church with Mark's parents. My parents must not have stayed for coffee, because they were nowhere to be seen. We headed to Mark's house to eat Sunday dinner and relax all afternoon. Mark and I had a lot of catching up to do and plans to make for their future together.

At the house, I helped Joy with dinner by setting the table. Joy had a roast, potatoes, and carrots in the slow cooker, which smelled great when we entered the house. We talked while we finalized the meal. Everyone was very hungry, and we talked and laughed happily as the meal was devoured.

Joy put a hand on my arm as I attempted to clear the table. "I will do this cleaning up. You and Mark have things to discuss, so why don't you two take a walk or sit in the living room and do some serious catching up."

"Okay, but we have all afternoon," I replied thoughtfully.

"You two deserve some time alone, so go. Amy is here to help," Joy said in her motherly way that always made me feel at home.

Mark and I left to take a walk down the road, with our arms around each other. Neither felt like talking at that moment, just enjoying the closeness and being together after four years of not spending much together time.

"Mark, I feel like I'm in heaven, having you home for good. I have waited for this day for so long, and it's finally here. Pinch me, I think I might be dreaming," I said as we walked with our arms around each other.

"I know what you mean. We have waited for this day for so long. It is real. I'm home for good, and I promise to never leave you again," Mark said to me as he stopped and pulled me into a hug, and then he kissed me like he had never kissed me before. There was more passion and love than I had ever felt.

When Mark broke the kiss, he whispered in my ear, "I love you so much!"

I smiled at him and said, "I love you too. I will always love you and follow you to the end of the world."

With that, we joined hands and started back to the house to deal with our wedding plans.

Chapter 14

When Mark and I returned home, we figured we better got out the list of wedding preparations I had half put together. Mark and I were planning on getting married in three months, on September 15.

"Okay, what do you have so far?" Mark asked, not aware of all it took to put on a wedding.

"We have the date and the church. We need to decide if we want music or not, and if so, do we want the organ for the music? Are we going to have a reception, cake, photographer, dance?" I sadly had to remind Mark that I couldn't ask my parents to pay for anything. I had saved up about three thousand since I had started my job at the clinic. I hadn't spent a dime more than I needed to, packing my lunch every day and not buying anything unnecessarily. But most of that money needed to go to renting or buying a house, furnishing a house, and whatever else came up. We had almost three more months to save for the wedding.

"Don't you think your parents would want to be a part of their only daughter's wedding?" Mark already knew the answer to that question but asked anyway.

When I was six years old, I had gone shopping with my mom and dad. I found a doll I really wanted. I was begging and whining and pouting. Finally, Bob, my dad, yelled at me and told me, "*No*, we are looking for a gift for your cousin, not you." I couldn't understand why I couldn't have a little doll. I kept asking, and my father was getting upset with me. Finally, he lost his patience and told me no and to never ask for anything ever again.

I was devastated that my father had yelled at me in front of other customers in the store and not let me have the doll. I was really embarrassed. I fell silent immediately and said not another word all the way home. When I got home, I went to my room and remained there until suppertime. I sadly ate a little supper, although no one noticed. I could not forgive my father, and I remained very angry with him. After that, I never asked my parents for anything.

Now I couldn't believe I let something so trivial to come between me and my parents. Now it seemed very immature to let something so ridiculous make such a big influence on my life. But at six years of age, it seemed like the end of the world.

"Mark, you know I can't ask my parents to pay for our wedding." I couldn't help feeling some regret for the whole situation. "If we can't afford to pay for everything, we could just have the ceremony at the church and that will be it. All we need is to get married, right? I would not feel right getting married anywhere but God's house. How do you feel about it, Mark?"

"I definitely want a church wedding too," Mark remarked. He waited for a while and then went on, "Katie, don't you want a fairy-tale wedding with the fancy dress, flowers, lots of pictures, reception, cake, and dancing? Doesn't every little girl dream of that?" Mark felt so bad for my situation with my parents.

I had gone into depression and treatment when I was thirteen years old. Dr. Wells had recognized the symptoms of depression and had sent me to see Dr. Carol Simpson. I really liked her. She was very soft-spoken, and I felt I could talk to her. She did sessions with Mom and Dad to explain what the problems seemed to be and find out how they viewed our home lives. Mom didn't seem to think there was a problem.

Dad said he thought I was sad sometimes, but he thought it was just being a girl with hormones.

Dr. Simpson told them that I wasn't able to get my schoolwork done because of all the work I had to do around the house. She suggested that they lighten the load for me so I could get my homework done and get adequate sleep. Also, she asked if Mom took me shopping for my clothes or took me to the grocery store to be a part of the purchasing of our food. Mom told her, "No, I just do it myself."

Dr. Simpson told her that I felt very left out of the loop. "You need to involve her in the shopping. Take her to the store and let her pick out her own clothes. It's important to girls to look somewhat like the rest of the girls at school. Do you know the kids are making fun of her at school because of her clothes and the fact that she doesn't have many? Something needs to change with your daughter or you're going to lose her."

Dad was willing to change things at home. He was going to have Greg and Dan help more in the house, and he was going to try to come in from the barn to help with supper. Mark was by my side as much as he could be, holding my hand and reassuring me. He even went into some of the sessions with me. It helped, but I still couldn't bring myself to ask my parents for anything.

They didn't seem to pay much attention to me as I grew up. If I hadn't had Mark, Amy, and their parents, I don't know if I would have survived my teenage years. They took pride in their boys and left me in the background. I was told to do a lot of the housework and hardly ever got a thanks for anything I did. There were at least two Christmases that I didn't even get a present from my parents. I was always unhappy and kept to myself and hung out in my room when I wasn't doing the cooking, cleaning, or laundry.

If I hadn't had Amy, Mark, and their parents, I would have been a lost soul. Amy and Mark had caught me crying many times and tried to do whatever they could to make me happy. Mark promised me when I was fifteen years old that he would take me away from my sad life when he got older and make me very happy. I wanted to believe that it would happen, but that was so far into the future it was hard to grasp.

"Katie, come back to me." Mark was snapping his fingers to get my attention back to the present. "Are you going to at least ask your dad to give you away?" Mark didn't know if he dared to ask me.

"I don't know if he would even if I did ask," I reluctantly said. "I guess if he volunteers, I will let him. But I won't ask him even though we are talking more now."

"Okay, what else? You mentioned music. I could sing a song to you." Mark beamed with a shy smile. Mark was a good singer, so that would be nice. "Or we could sing a song together. I know you can sing. I have heard you at church, and you sang in choir at school. We still need music for the processional and our escape."

"The escape? What's that supposed to mean?" I asked with wonder. "We could have the organist play those, I suppose."

"Okay, the organist it is. I was just teasing you about the escape, lighten up, will you? The escape is when we can rush off to be by ourselves. What else? You mentioned a reception and cake. I don't think we can afford to pay for a reception and a cake. I haven't even found a job yet. I don't know what to tell you there. Instead of a reception, why don't we just take the few guests we will invite and the wedding party out to dinner and call it good? Maybe Mom can make us a nice cake that we could eat at the restaurant. What about that? It's just a suggestion. If you don't like it, just say so." Mark was hoping to make me as happy as I could be on my wedding day.

"What about rings? Are we going to have matching bands?" I asked hopefully.

"I have your ring, remember, I bought it with the engagement ring. I got a better deal that way. I don't need a ring right away, I guess, but it would be nice to show the whole world that I belong to you," Mark expressed.

"We could go look and see if we could afford a ring. I would love for you to wear my ring," I said with tears stinging my eyes.

"All right, let's tell your parents what we want to do for the wedding." I didn't sound all that happy. After all, this was supposed to be my day, and we couldn't afford to have all the glamour most weddings had.

After we told Joy and Paul about our plans, not sounding very excited about the supposedly happy day, we looked at each other, hoping everything would work out.

Paul and Joy gave each other a long, loving look and were quiet for a while. "Is this really what you two want, or is this all you can afford right now?"

"Joy and Paul, you know the history with my father, and you know I can't ask him for any help with the wedding. If you want better for your son, I will step aside, and he can find a woman worthy of your name and reputation. I don't know if my family supports me in this marriage, but I can't ask them to pay for this." I got up and ran from the room and out of the house. Mark knew I was crying, and with a deep sigh, he went after me.

I was a ways down the road when Mark caught up with me. "Hold up, Katie, we need to talk this through. My parents didn't mean you weren't worthy of me or our name. They only want the best for us, and they want to help us have a really nice wedding. They didn't know if you would accept help from them, so they haven't said anything. Come back so they can tell you their suggestions. You don't have to accept it if you don't want to. Come on back. I don't like seeing you upset like this. Come on, sweetheart, we can work through this."

Back at the house, Paul and Joy were waiting patiently for our return. They both hugged me and asked us to have a seat.

"We wanted to offer to pay for a reception with cake, pictures, and a dance. We have always loved you like our own daughter. We want you and Mark to have a wedding you will remember for the rest of your life. So plan for a lovely wedding that you want, and we'll make sure that it is paid for."

"I love you two like my parents too." I was starting to cry again. This was all too much. "You do know it's not your responsibility to pay for our wedding, don't you? You have Amy's wedding to pay for in July, how can you afford to help us too?"

"We certainly do have Amy's wedding to pay for, but Mark is our son, and you are as good as our daughter. We want to do this for you two. You both deserve all the happiness in the world," Paul said in a very loving, fatherly voice. "Why don't you think about it and get back to us?"

Tired of wedding talk, Mark and I decided to pop in a DVD to watch and take our minds off the wedding. I curled up close to Mark, and soon we were both fast asleep.

Chapter 15

Monday morning Mark called Ray Sherburn Law Firm in Des Moines. Ray was a longtime lawyer in Des Moines, a friend of Paul's, and very well-known. Mark was going to ask if he could do a year of internship with their firm. Ray had a partner, Calvin Harris, who was younger than Ray but very good too. It would be an honor to work with both Ray and Calvin.

Ray was very happy to hear from Mark. "Why don't you come in this morning and we will discuss this?" They said their good-byes, and Mark showered and got ready to go into town.

Ray met Mark at the door with a big smile and handshake. "Come in. I'm so glad you called," Ray exclaimed. "I had talked to your dad the other day, and he told me you were about done with school. If I didn't hear from you, I was going to call you and offer you an internship here. We have been really busy, and I could use an extra hand. Plus next year, my wife wants us to take a cruise to Alaska. We will be gone a whole month. I can't tell you how hard that will be to do if I don't have someone I can rely on to cover my job. I will look over your résumé, and I will get back to you very soon, probably tomorrow. I'm sure I will like what I'll see, since I hear you graduated at the top of your class. If everything looks as good as I think it will, I would like to offer you a permanent partnership with our firm."

Mark was so excited he could hardly contain himself. They talked for about a half hour, catching up on each other's lives. "How is Susan and your son and daughter?" Mark asked. "Dad told me Greg is following in your footsteps after all. What made him change his mind?"

"Susan is doing very well. She works really hard at the hospital and keeping me in line," Ray said laughingly. "It is so nice of you to ask. Susan has been head of obstetrics at Southern Memorial Hospital for twenty years. Families love her very dearly.

"Greg decided he didn't like teaching like he thought he would, so he switched over to law. He has two years of school left. He says this is what he should have gone into in the first place. Sometimes it takes a while to figure out what you want to do. I can tell you something though, I'm glad he came to his senses and chose law." Ray seemed very proud of his son. "Sheila is in France, studying art. She does a lot of painting and goes to a lot of art shows. She plans to be home in a year or so. We haven't seen her in a while, and we miss her very much. We're hoping she can fly home for Christmas this year."

"Sounds like your family leads very busy lives. You sound very proud of them, as you should. I can't wait to meet with Greg. I haven't seen him for quite a few years. When we were in high school, I always looked up to him. He was a leader back then, and I bet he hasn't changed. Is Sheila as pretty as she was in high school? She sure could turn the boys' heads. If I hadn't had Katie, I might have chased after her myself. Say hello to Susan for me. I look forward to seeing her again in person some time. Thank you for the chance to work here at your firm. I know I will enjoy being taught by the best." Mark stood up and met Ray halfway around his desk, and they shook hands, and Mark left the office. His feet hardly touched the ground as he walked to the car. This would be a great firm to work for.

I called Mark on my lunch hour. I knew Mark was going to call Ray this morning. "Hi, sweetheart!" Mark sounded full of happiness. "I talked to Ray, and I can do my internship with him, and I have a good chance of joining his firm permanently."

"That is wonderful news! When will you know?" I asked with equal enthusiasm. "I know we want to save our money, but I would like to celebrate your probable job. Maybe we could do a picnic down by the river where we like to go? It wouldn't cost too much, we have to eat anyway."

"Okay. I will go to the store, get some food, and have it ready when you get off work. I will be in the parking lot waiting for you. See you in a few hours." Mark was so thoughtful, and I loved him so much.

I walked out of the clinic at five thirty, and Mark was waiting for me in the parking lot. Mark was all smiles as he got out of his car and went around to open the door for me. "We can pick your car up later," Mark said.

We drove to our favorite spot by the river, where there was a lovely picnic area. Mark had a big picnic basket in the backseat. "You must have bought out the store," I teased him. "Something smells really good, and I am starving."

Mark seemed really quiet as we drove to the beach area. I looked at him with some anxiety. "You're really quiet tonight, what's wrong?"

When we reached to spot we were going to, Mark took my hands in his and looked into my eyes. "I have something to tell you before we eat." My heart almost stopped, and I must have looked a little pale, because Mark sat me down on the blanket. "It's nothing bad. Ray called me, and I got the job at his firm after my internship! Isn't that wonderful, Katie? Of course I will just be doing my internship for a year, but I'm in. I start tomorrow morning. I can't wait to get my feet wet, as they say."

"That is wonderful! You scared me half to death. I thought something terrible had happened. Don't do that again!" I could now start to breathe again. I hadn't realized I had been holding my breath.

Mark and I relaxed and enjoyed our picnic supper Mark had packed. We talked about our upcoming plans and our hopes and dreams. Things seemed to be coming together quite well.

About seven o'clock, we packed up our supper and headed for the store to do some shopping for Mark's big day tomorrow. We thought some new clothes would make Mark look more professional for the office.

Chapter 16

Amy called Saturday morning to ask if I could go shopping with her; her mother; her future sister-in-law, Sherry; April, my sister-in-law; and my mother that afternoon. We had to look for bridesmaid dresses and some things for Amy's bridal shower, which was next Saturday. Sherry and I had been planning the shower for a while. We agreed to go that afternoon.

"I am taking all of you to lunch at the mall so we have enough strength for our shopping," Amy informed me. "Sherry is meetings us there, so do you and your mom want to meet us at the mall at eleven thirty? Your mom said she would pick April up." April and Amy were my bridesmaids.

"That sounds good. I just have to shower quickly, and we will be there. Mom actually wanted to come shopping with us? I'm surprised at that. See you in an hour," I said very happily.

When we arrived at the mall, we headed for the food court to get some lunch. This was going to be such fun. I hadn't shopped with my mom since I was five years old. We ordered our food and sat down to eat before shopping. We decided on which shops to browse through, and after eating, we headed to the first store.

We shopped and shopped, finally finding dresses we all liked. We tried on funky ones and laughed and laughed. I never knew shopping could be such fun. Amy's color was peach for her bridesmaids, and mine was a dusty rose. We had trouble finding peach, so Amy decided to go with a light pink. That we found right away. Sherry and I loved the dresses we found, and they were on clearance. I could handle that.

We also found the rose-colored dresses for Amy and April in the clearance section. This was going better than we could have expected.

"Katie, we are having such good luck today, why don't we look for your wedding dress? You have a lot of help." Joy suggested.

"Okay, I guess it won't hurt," I said to the ladies. "Let's look in the bargain section first. I hate to spend a lot of money on a dress to wear one day." We found a few and headed to the bride's dressing room. I loved one dress in particular. The style was just what I liked. When I got the gown on, all the women said, "*Ahh!*"

"That's the dress for you. You look beautiful in it, and I don't think you will need any alterations," Mom said, admiring the dress. "Do you like it?"

"I love the way I look in it. Do you think it looks better than the other ones? The price is only $300. I was expecting to spend a lot more than that," I said as we tried to decide if I should get the dress or not.

Joy pulled my hair up on my head and said, "With your hair up, the dress looks very elegant, Katie. I think you should get it. Do you girls have anything to say about the dress?"

The girls agreed that that was the dress. I got out of the dress and felt happy at having found the dress of my dreams.

Amy suggested, "Let's look for dresses for the mothers of the brides also. You ladies need to look as lovely as the rest of the bridal party." So we started to look for more dresses for Joy and Mom. Our moms had fun looking and trying on dress after dress until they found the right ones.

Then we headed to the shoe section to get shoes to match the color of our gowns. We were all very tired of shopping but were glad it was done. With bags in hand, we headed outside to put our purchases into our cars.

When we met back inside the mall, Sherry said, "We still have to pick up decorations and prizes for Amy's shower." So we headed to a party store that was in the mall. We found what we were looking for and headed for the food court again.

We were tired, but I didn't want this wonderful shopping day to end. I didn't go shopping very often because I was saving as much money as I could.

We ordered drinks and two orders of nachos to munch on. We all agreed that the shopping day had been very successful. At five o'clock we hugged, said good-bye, and departed to our own houses.

Chapter 17

By the time Saturday rolled around, both Mark and I were ready for a couple of days off. We had an appointment with a realtor to go house hunting. Mark picked me up at nine o'clock to meet Mrs. Jenkins in town. Mrs. Jenkins, a real estate agent, was a friend of Joy's and had arranged for her to show us some houses. They had been friends for years and knew she would find us the perfect house.

We looked at several houses, and by one o'clock, we were at the last one on Mrs. Jenkins's list. It was a four-bedroom, two baths, and a big fenced-in backyard in a very nice neighborhood. It looked in very good shape. The realtor said the family that owned it had to move away for the husband's job and wanted to sell quickly, so the asking price was very reasonable.

The house was very nice, and we both loved it. Now for the price! Mark and I couldn't believe our ears when the realtor told us the price. It was the best offer we had had all day. We could keep looking, but we really liked this one. Mark and I looked at each other, and we realized this was the one.

"All right," Mark and I said at the same time, jumping up and down. We couldn't believe it. We headed to Mrs. Jenkins's office to work out the details of the purchase. We wouldn't be closing on the house until August 15. The owners were moving by the fifteenth. They would be packed and on the road after closing. We had a whole house to decorate and furnish. What fun we would have. We left Mrs. Jenkins's office with great excitement. We talked a mile a minute about what we each liked about the house, and we couldn't think of anything we didn't like. We couldn't wait to tell Joy and Paul about the house.

We drove to Mark's house, as we were having Amy's bridal shower at five o'clock. Mark, Phil, Steve, and Paul were going to go play golf during the shower. Joy, Amy, Sherry, and Mark's two grandmothers were busy in the kitchen, getting the food ready. The living room was decorated, and everything looked fabulous. "I'm sorry I wasn't more help to you today, but we did find a wonderful house. Mark and I would like to set up an appointment so you and Paul can look at the house in case we missed something. We couldn't find anything wrong with the house. You all did a great job decorating the house, it looks wonderful," I told the ladies.

Soon the guest showed up, and it was a very exciting shower. We served food, played a few games, and Amy opened her gifts. Amy was a little embarrassed when she opened her gift from Sherry. Sherry had bought her a very sexy nightie. We all had a good laugh over it and told her she should model it for us. She said, "No, this is for my husband." Phil and Amy received many wonderful items for their home. I helped clean up since I wasn't there for the beginning. Soon the guys arrived home, and Amy had to show Phil all the gifts they had received. She was so excited. "I have one more gift, but you can't see it until our wedding night." All the men groaned, and Amy was embarrassed all over again. Then we sat on the patio and visited for a while. It had been a very gratifying day, and Mark drove me home.

Chapter 18

On Monday, Mark called Mrs. Jenkins to see if he could set up an appointment for Joy and Paul go look at the house. Mark and I also thought it would be a good gesture to ask my mom and dad to look at the house too. The appointment was set up for the following Saturday morning. Much to my surprise, Mom and Dad were overjoyed to go take a look at the house that we had chosen and be a part of our lives.

Mom and Dad followed Joy and Paul to the house. We had gone ahead to meet Mrs. Jenkins at the house. Our parents were excited as they strolled through the house. They were overjoyed with the purchase. They offered some suggestions for decorating, which I wanted to consider because Mom didn't often offer me help. They were very pleased with the condition of the house. "This is going to be so much fun picking out furniture and wall hangings." Joy was as excited as I was. Feeling very good about the house, they thanked Mrs. Jenkins for showing the house to all of them. We could move in anytime after closing on August 15.

"You could live in the house if you wanted to after we get it ready to live in," Mark offered to me.

"I think we should both move in together after the wedding. That will make it seem more special, don't you think?" I told Mark. "I can't wait to live here as your wife and you as my husband. We can paint, decorate, and buy some furniture for the house in the meantime so after the wedding, we could just go to our new house and start our lives together. This is so exciting!"

Chapter 19

Amy's wedding arrived in no time. Everyone was busy getting to where they needed to be. Sherry and I helped Amy get dressed, and then we put our dresses on. We had had our hair done earlier in the day, so that was done. We just had to do our makeup, and we would be ready. After the photographer took some pictures in the dressing room, it was time to head for the door to walk down the aisle. I was as nervous as Amy was. "Take deep breaths," I kept telling myself.

Sherry and Mike walked down the aisle first. Then I looked at Mark, and he looked at me, and we were lost in our own world. Suddenly, we realized where we were and what we were supposed to be doing. Then I took Mark's arm to be escorted down the aisle. Mark bent down to me and whispered, "You look very beautiful!" I smiled from ear to ear as we headed to the front of the church. I felt what Cinderella must have felt. I couldn't stop smiling.

Finally, the music changed, everyone stood, and Amy and Paul walked to the front of the church. Amy was very beautiful, and I was honored to be her maid of honor. Phil was to be Amy's husband, and you could tell how much he loved her. There was so much love in the air I was sure everyone could feel it. In a couple of months, it would be us up there. I had never been in a wedding before. It was all so exciting. I hope our wedding would be as wonderful as Amy and Phil's was turning out to be.

Phil and Amy exchanged their vows. Mark was asked to sing for the ceremony. The love song he sang was amazing. I felt like he was singing it to me. Then they lit the unity candle to join their bodies as one.

When they returned to stand in front of the minister, Pastor Bailey announced them husband and wife. Phil took Amy into his arms and kissed her with great affection. As Amy and Phil turned to face their guests, they were introduced for the first time as Mr. and Mrs. Mallery. Everyone stood and clapped as Phil and Amy made their way back down the aisle to the fellowship hall. Mark and I followed, and then Sherry and Mike followed us.

Phil's parents and Joy and Paul were in the reception line as guests filed through, wishing the bride and groom the best.

After we left the church, Phil, Amy, Sherry, Mike, Mark, and I rode around town in their decorated car. People honked their horn at us and cheered. We waved and yelled back at them. It was great fun.

We were due to be at the restaurant at five o'clock, so we headed for Willow Creek Inn for the reception and dance to follow. As we entered, we could hear the band playing some soft music. All the guests were mingling and talking, enjoying a great evening out.

When the leader of the band saw we were there, he hushed the crowd and asked them to find their seats so the meal could be served. As quiet fell, he said, "We will begin by bringing in the wedding party. The first couple is Phil's sister, Sherri, and her husband Mike. The best man is Amy's brother, Mark, and his fiancée, Katie. Will you all help me to welcome the bride and groom, Mr. and Mrs. Phil Mallery." Everyone clapped and cheered. When they got to their table, everyone was clanking their glasses for the bride and groom to kiss. Of course they didn't hesitate. The evening was so magical.

The dance started at seven o'clock, with Amy and Phil dancing their first dance as man and wife. Then Amy and Paul danced the traditional father-daughter dance. At last, it was time for the bridal party to dance. Mark took me into his arms. It was wonderful. I really did feel like Cinderella then. Except I knew I wouldn't turn into a pumpkin at midnight. I would go home without Mark, but I knew my life was all good. Mark loved me, and I loved him.

Chapter 20

One night after supper, my dad approached me and asked if I needed some money to pay for the wedding. "You haven't asked for any help. The bride's parents usually pay for the wedding." I was so surprised I couldn't speak. At last Dad said, "I can pay for the reception, dance, and photographer. I hear you have your dress. Are there any expenses at the church? If there is anything else you need help with, let me know. I would also like to give you away. After all, you are the only daughter I have." Dad looked at me very lovingly and with hope in his eyes.

I told Dad, "It would be great if you help pay for the wedding. We weren't going to go too extravagant because we didn't have the money for all of it. Mark is just starting his job after college, and we haven't been able to save too much. It would be wonderful to have a nice wedding like most girls have, but we can keep it pretty small. Why don't I have Mark come over so we can let you know what we have in mind?"

I called Mark, and he came right over. We told Dad and Mom what we wanted for our wedding, and they agreed that it was very affordable. "We can make this a very lovely wedding for my little girl," Dad said lovingly.

"Thank you, Dad." I was overcome with emotion. We hugged, and he told me to give him the bills when they came in. I was very grateful that Dad was helping us with the expenses. *I guess he does love me after all. If only he could have shown some of that love when I was growing up. I needed his love back then as much as I need it now. He was just so busy making a living on the farm that he didn't have the time, I guess. Maybe he realizes he made a mistake back then and is trying to make up for it. I am just glad he is finally finding his way back into my life.*

"Have you sent out invitations yet? We should invite all our relatives and friends, don't you think?" Mom asked. "I have the list of relatives and friends from Jeff's wedding. We can use the same list. Let me get it."

When Mom came back into the living room, she showed us the list. It was a lot more people than we had planned on inviting, but if they wanted to invite them, who were we to argue. "Do you need help addressing the invitations?" Mom asked.

I said, "That would be nice to have some help with all that writing and stamp licking. I would appreciate the help. Thank you. We picked out the invitation we liked but didn't know how many to order. Maybe we can figure that out tonight so I can order them tomorrow."

I was so happy my mom wanted to help with the invitations.

Chapter 21

One Saturday morning, Mark, Joy, Paul, Mom, Dad, and I decided go shopping for paint for our bedroom and the living room. We all thought the living room would look best done in warm shades of cream, tan, brown, and some country blue for color. We browsed the paint selection and decided on a warm cream color.

Mark and I decided we would like a dusty rose color for our bedroom, and we could accent with cream and pinks. We would look for a bedspread later.

The Olsens had moved out the week before, making the house empty, so we decided to start the painting right away. With all of us there to tape, paint around the doors, windows, ceiling, and floorboards, we decided to split up and paint both the bedroom and the living room. With all the help, we were done in three hours. The rooms looked great.

Since no one felt like cooking, we decided to go out for dinner to cap off the great day we had had together. After church and dinner on Sunday, we decided to go furniture shopping. We thought we should check out four different furniture stores and compare prices.

We found a great dining room table with two leaves and six chairs right away. Then we went looking for living room furniture and bedroom furniture. We had good luck and found things on sale. We even found living room lamps. The furniture would be delivered on Wednesday late in the afternoon. Mark said he could be at the house at five o'clock.

I was surprised at how we were able to make our money stretch. After buying a bedroom set, living room furniture, a dining room table and chairs, we still had quite a bit of money left. There was a stove, washer, dryer, and dishwasher in the house that were fairly new. We could use them as they looked relatively new. We would wait until after the wedding to see what we didn't get and purchase the rest of the necessaries then. We would get a lot of items for my bridal shower. We would also have wedding gifts to fit into the house. The house was really beginning to look like home.

I liked the location of this house because we were only four blocks from Amy and Phil's house. We could walk to each other's house. Amy and Phil's house was a four-level split with a three-car garage and a big fenced-in backyard. The landscaping was professionally done and looked gorgeous. Our house was a colonial style with a three-car garage and a big fenced-in backyard. We also had a gazebo in the backyard. Both yards had plenty of room for our children to run and play in someday in the future. Neither Amy nor I wanted to have children for a couple of years. We wanted to have time to get ahead financially and have time to enjoy personal time together before children arrived. We probably would even get a dog someday. All children love having a dog, and they were great playmates.

Chapter 22

A week before the wedding, my bridal shower was scheduled to take place. It was being held at Amy's house. Mom and I drove to Amy's house way before the guests were supposed to arrive. The house was decorated very nicely. Mark was there, and I asked, "What are you doing here? I didn't know the guys were invited to the shower."

"Phil, Dad, Steve, and I are going to play golf. I just wanted to see you for a few minutes before I left. Do you want to go to a movie after the shower?" Mark asked.

"Sure, that would be wonderful. I think it might be over by eight thirty or so. Will you be back by then?" I asked Mark.

"I'll make sure I am." Mark kissed me and left with Phil. "You ladies have fun."

We had a big group of women that came. I was surprised that I had so many friends, and a lot of relatives came too. We played several games, and it was so much fun. Then I opened my gifts. I got so many wonderful items for the house. When I thought I was done, Amy said she had one more for me. She handed me a gift box with a big bow on it. I opened it to find a sexy negligee in it. I was a little embarrassed, but then I thought, *This is all women, so what.* We all laughed, and Amy said I needed to model it. I said, "I don't think so. This is for my man only."

Then April and Amy served a supper of sandwiches, chips, salads, and cake. Everything tasted wonderful. When we were about done eating, the men showed up and ate too. They said they were starved and made short work of the extra food. Needless to say, we didn't have much to put away.

I showed all the wonderful gifts to Mark, and Amy said, "Katie got a very special gift from me, but she wouldn't model it for us."

Mark looked at me with a grin on his face and asked, "Will you model it for me? I hope it is something sexy."

"Not until our wedding night," I told Mark with a sexy smile on my face. "You will have to let your imagination run until then."

After everyone left, Mark and I loaded the gifts into the car and headed for the house to put them away. Then we headed to the movies. It was nice to relax with my head on Mark's shoulder and watch a chick flick.

"Why did you pick this movie? You don't like these kinds of movies that much," I asked as we left the theater.

"Who said I was watching the movie? I just like watching and being close to you," Mark said with heat in his eyes.

Hand in hand, we walked to Mark's car. "This has been such a wonderful day, and you made it very special for me by taking me to a movie. Thank you," I told Mark as he opened the door for me.

After Mark got behind the wheel, he asked, "Do you want to get a bite to eat before we head home?"

"Sure, I don't want this evening to end. It has been great. Where are we going?" I asked.

"Let's go to Perkins. I have something to discuss with you before the wedding. It's nothing bad, but I think we should discuss it just the same," Mark informed me.

As it turned out, Mark just wanted to make sure all the wedding plans were coming together and if my dad had come through for me. "I just don't want any surprises after the wedding. I would rather know now if we have some financial dilemma going on," Mark told me.

"No need to worry. My dad has paid for everything. He has been great! I am so happy Dad and even Mom have a fairly good relationship with me now," I said to Mark.

We just had a cup of coffee at the restaurant, but it was nice and relaxing. Then Mark and I headed to his car to go home.

Chapter 23

Our big weekend was finally here! On Friday night, we went to the rehearsal at the church, which was uneventful. Then we headed to Joy and Paul's house for a big backyard barbecue. There were horseshoes, volleyball, and croquet to play. It was a fun evening, with music filling the warm summer air.

The next morning, Mom, Joy, Amy, and I met at the hair salon to get our hair done. I was so nervous I could hardly sit still. At last my big day had arrived. "Stop your fidgeting," Carol, my hair stylist, said to me. She was laughing as she said it, so I knew she was teasing. "I don't think I have ever seen such a nervous bride, except maybe Amy when she got married."

"I think all brides are nervous. It's only natural because it is a big step in a girl's life. I wasn't that bad was I?" Amy asked sympathetically.

"You were quite nervous too," Carol said. "I practically had to run around the room to catch up with your hair."

"Oh, I wasn't that bad. I was nervous, but I stayed in my seat, I know that," Amy defended herself.

By three o'clock, we arrived at the church to get dressed. My dress had been delivered and was hanging in the dressing room when I walked in. It was gorgeous! It was even prettier than when I had seen it the first time. I couldn't believe I would be wearing this beautiful gown.

Amy helped me get into the dress, and we found the flowers to be passed out to moms, dads, grandparents, and the wedding party. The air was filled with the scent of lily of the valley and mauve roses.

Amy and April were also very beautiful in their rose-colored gowns. Amy appeared to be very calm. "Oh, Amy, how did you get through your wedding day? I am so nervous! I'm sweating through my dress." For being the middle of September, it was unusually warm. Joy found a fan to help keep me from passing out. That helped a lot.

At three forty-five, the photographer came in to take some dressing shots and nervous shots. The ceremony would start at four o'clock. "Oh God, let me not pass out or do anything dumb," I prayed.

At last, Amy and April were ushered to the door of the church, where they would meet up with Steve and Greg. The music started, and April and Greg made their way to the front of the church. Then it was Amy and Steve's turn to make their way down the aisle.

Finally, my dad appeared at my door and took my arm to escort me down the aisle. "Are you ready? You look like a princess. I am so proud to be giving you away today. Let's do this, shall we?" With a big smile, I took his arm, and the music rose, and we walked arm in arm down the aisle to the front where Mark stood. I looked at all the people and thought, *This is a very good day.*

When I got to the front of the church, the minister asked, "Who gives this woman away?"

Dad said, "Her mother and I do." With a smile on his face, Dad gave my arm to Mark, and we made our way to stand in front of the minister. We looked into each other's eyes, and my nerves vanished. Pastor Bailey said a few words for the bride and groom, we exchanged vows, and rings were placed on our fingers. Then it was time for the music. Mark and I sang "From This Moment On" to each other. I wasn't even nervous. The only other person in the church was Mark. Then we lit the unity candle and were pronounced husband and wife.

Mark bent to kiss me as our family and friends clapped and yelled with joy.

As we turned toward our guests, Pastor Bailey said, "I am proud to introduce you to Mr. and Mrs. Mark Johnson."

Everyone stood and cheered as Mark and I made our way to the fellowship hall, where our family and friends congratulated us. Amy and Steve followed us out, and April and Greg followed them. Our parents joined us in the reception line, and it was wonderful to see everyone.

The photographer was ready to do our still shots, so we gathered everyone at the front of the church for those. In no time, those were done, and we could proceed to the reception hall.

The reception and dance were at the Willow Creek Inn a few blocks away. Mark had been in charge of decorating the hall. It was magnificent! There were flowers and candles everywhere. "This is fabulous, Mark! You did a good job." I was so proud of my new husband.

"Steve and Phil helped a lot. They have had experience in this department. The people from the inn helped a lot too. It was actually a lot of fun. I might have missed my calling," Mark said teasingly. We waited in a room off the dining room until we could be announced. When the band leader knew we had arrived, he motioned for the guests to find their seats and quiet down so the meal could be served.

When everyone was seated and quiet, the bandleader said, "I would like to introduce you to the Johnson wedding party." He announced April and Greg then Amy and Steve. "Now I would like to introduce you to Mr. and Mrs. Mark Johnson." We smiled at each other and made our grand entrance. Everyone stood up and cheered. This was such a magnificent group of people. We felt very blessed to have so many friends and family.

We ate a very lavish dinner of chicken, wild rice, and vegetables. Our friends and family hardly let us eat. They wanted us to kiss all during dinner, but neither of us seemed to hesitate whenever the clanking began.

Mark and I made our way to the cake to cut the first piece. That was a messy job. Mark threatened to smash a piece of it into my face. I gave him a warning look that said, "Don't you dare." I was glad he took me seriously. I didn't want cake all over my dress. We had the dance to get through yet.

At seven o'clock, the dance started. The leader of the band announced that the first dance would be danced by the bride and groom. "This first dance is a dedication from the groom to the bride. Mr. and Mrs. Mark Johnson, will you please take the floor." Mark led me onto the dance floor, and we fell into each other's arms. It was wonderful as we swayed around the room to the music Mark had chosen for our first dance together. We gazed into each other's eyes with so much love.

Then it was announced that the next number was to be danced by the bride and her father. I started to panic! What if Dad didn't want to dance with me? Then I thought I was being silly. Of course he would dance with me. It was hard to believe things had changed so much between Dad and me. Out of the corner of my eye, I saw Dad make his way to me. He held out his hand and took me onto the dance floor. We danced to "Daddy's Hands" with such feeling, and he looked like he really loved me.

As the dance ended, Dad escorted me over to Mark. But before he handed me back, he looked into my eyes and said with the deepest love I had ever seen, "You are truly my princess tonight! I couldn't be more proud of my little girl than I am today. You have grown up to be a very beautiful woman." With that, he bent down and hugged and kissed me. As I clung to him, I had tears in my eyes because I knew my father truly loved me.

Then the wedding party danced the next dance. Paul caught me as I was exiting the dance floor. "May I have this dance, daughter-in-law?" He held out his hand, and I took it with the love I had had for Paul all my life. "You sure look beautiful tonight. This has been a fairy-tale wedding. I hope this has been everything you had dreamed of."

"To tell you the truth, this has been much more than I could have imagined. It has been wonderful. I feel like Cinderella at the ball," I said with a laugh.

I danced with everyone at least once. I hadn't danced so much in my life. I really felt like a fairy-tale princess who had found her prince. Mark and I danced and danced. Mark whispered sweet things into my ear as we danced. "Why don't we do that escape thing? I am getting really anxious for our wedding night to start."

"Honey, we can't leave this early. Besides, we haven't thrown the bouquet and my garter yet. It would be impolite if we left before the dance ended. The band is playing until eleven o'clock. We should be able to leave then."

"Okay, I just want to be alone with you. This has been a wonderful wedding, don't you think?" Mark asked as we danced.

"It has been more than I ever thought I would have. There are so many people here. Look at all the gifts on the tables. I think we will have our house full. You ready to throw my garter?" I asked Mark.

"Oh, I think that is a good idea." Mark and I made our way to the stage, where the band would inform our guests that it was time to throw the garter and bouquet before too many people left.

The band leader announced that all single men should gather around for the tossing of the garter. I sat on a chair, and Mark used his mouth and teeth to get my garter off my leg. Everyone was cheering as Mark got ready to throw the garter. He turned around twice, and with his back to the crowd, he threw the garter to the crowd.

Then the band leader announced for all single girls to gather around for the tossing of the bouquet. I turned around twice and tossed my bouquet to the crowd. The girls scrambled to make a catch.

We danced a few more dances, and then it was almost time for the dance to end. It had been a long day, and Mark and I were tired. Soon our guests started to leave.

Amy, Steve, Craig, and April told us they would load up the gifts and take them to Amy's house. We were going to open them at Amy and Phil's house tomorrow. Our moms were making dinner, and then we would see what we received for gifts.

By eleven o'clock, most of the guests had left. We thanked the band for the wonderful job they had done. It was the same band Amy and Phil had at their dance. They did such a good job that Paul thought we should have them back for our dance. Because we had them twice, they said we could get them to play free for some future party we wanted to have. That sounded wonderful.

Mark and I said our good-byes to our parents, family, and friends who were still there. Then we made our way to our car to head for our house. We could have gone to a motel, but we had our house all set up to use, so we decided we would save money and stay at our home.

As we pulled into our garage, Mark came around the car to open my door and help me get out with my big skirt. We walked to the door leading into the house. All of a sudden, Mark picked me up in his arms, opened the door, and carried me over the threshold into the house. He bent to kiss me before putting me on my feet.

"You thought of everything didn't you?" I asked my husband. "You helped to make this the most special day of my life. I love you so much!"

"I wanted you to have that fairy-tale wedding I knew you have always wanted. I was happy to make that happen." With that, he took my hand, and we headed to the bedroom to try out our new bed.

Mark wanted to undress me, but he was having trouble getting my dress unbuttoned. I had to help him so we could get the job done tonight. After my dress was off, the rest of my clothes came off easier. Then I undressed Mark. I took my time, and Mark kept saying to hurry up. "You are so beautiful, and I can't wait any longer to run my hands over your body," Mark whispered to me.

At last we were both naked, and Mark started to kiss me, lay me on the bed, and he started to kiss me and run his hands over my breasts and suck on them. I was so aroused I could hardly lie still. I started to arch toward Mark and begging him to fill me with his warmth. He was having a hard time waiting too. At last he sunk deep inside me, and I was taken to a height I had never been before. After our climaxes, we were both breathing fast and hard. We had to rest for a few minutes before we could even talk. Making love with Mark was wonderful! Mark held me in his arms and curled a strand of my hair around his finger. "I am tired, but I don't want this night to end. It has been so wonderful. I really enjoyed dancing with you tonight, but I *really* enjoyed making love to you," Mark whispered in my ear.

"I enjoyed the dancing tonight too. I felt like what Cinderella must have felt at her ball. Most of all, I enjoyed making love with you. You were great! When can we do it again?" I asked Mark. "I don't think anyone has ever waited as long as we have to make love. I am surprised we made it."

We made love again after talking for a while, and we were both so tired we were ready to go to sleep. I whispered in Mark's ear as he lay almost asleep, "Good night, my prince! I love you! Thanks for rescuing me from a not-so-happy life and making me the happiest woman in the world."

As Mark cuddled me a little closer to him, he whispered into my ear, "I love you too! You have made me a very happy man too." Mark kissed me again and whispered, "Good night, Cinderella!"

About the Author

Lola May Groves was born in Dickinson, North Dakota, and now resides at her home in Dundas, Minnesota. She is retired from working as a cook for thirty years at two different nursing homes and enjoys traveling with her husband of forty-three years. Lola also enjoys cooking, reading, and sewing.

Lola has written a children's book prior to this publication entitled *My Birthday Pony*, which was also for sale in December. She plans on writing more children's books in the future.

Look forward to more publications of adult books in the coming years. This upcoming author has really enjoyed writing both a children's book as well as an adult book. Writing has been a passion of Lola's since she was a little girl.

Printed in the United States
By Bookmasters